ALWAYS
IN THE
CONVENT SHADOW

BY

MARGARET MATLEY

1991

ISBN 0-951-7265-0-1

Laserset by G. Beard & Son Ltd., Brighton, England.

Made and printed in Great Britain by
The Guernsey Press Co. Ltd., Guernsey, Channel Isles.

Published by Poppy Publications, England.

Distributed by Wolfhound Press,
68 Mountjoy Square, Dublin 1.

CONTENTS

Acknowledgements

The Reverend Bishop Delaney, R.I.P. Bishop of Cork 1870: The great and Holy man who turned his care into action.

James Hegarty, R.I.P., Lord Mayor of Cork 1870: May his name live on with gratitude in the hearts of all who love children.

Mr. Justice McCarthy, Children's Court, Dublin 1939: For his wisdom.

Reverend Mother Joseph: For her consent to use a reference on the Convent history. For her hospitality and good humour.

All the Nuns at Sunday's Well: For their hospitality and goodwill.

Sister Maura, The present School Directress: For all the old photos, and for recorded dates. For introducing the writer to the present day pupils. They radiated happiness. The School has undergone radical changes, all for the better. The children enjoy a happy and carefree life, along with thousands of school children in their City.

The children at Sunday's Well 1990: For their warm hospitality.

Richard, age 12 years: For the delicious chocolate cake that he baked.

Brother Raymond:
A dedicated professional for his hospitality.

Pat Cleary, Detective/Gárda: For his invaluable help to the author in researching addresses in Dublin.

Sheba, The present day children's alsation pet: For making friends with me.

SPECIAL ACKNOWLEDGEMENT

To Judith: For her invaluable help, editing and typing over many hours, day and night! Her diligence, dedication and relentless care warmly acknowledged by the author.

What Matters

One hundred
years from now,
it will not
matter
what kind of
car I drove,
what kind of
house I lived in,
how much I had
in my bank
account,
nor what my
clothes looked
like.

But the world
may be a little
better because
I was important
in the life
of a child.

Author Unknown

DEDICATIONS

To Peter, Colette and Dominique

Saint Mary Euphrasia:-

Mother Mary Eurphrasia was the daughter of a French Doctor. She was deeply concerned about young women in need of care and guidance. She joined an organisation of Nuns in Cont, France. The Order was that of St. John Eudes, the Sisters engaged in Charity work. But the young and energetic Sister Mary Euphrasia was not content to live in an Order that was almost enclosed. Each Convent of St. John Eudes was independent. Sister Mary Euphrasia left the Order and founded a new Order called the Sisters of the Good Shepherd. She stipulated that as new Convents opened around the world the Sisters would be part of every house. She created one large Congregation, closely linked in work and care under one governing headquarters at the Convent in Angers, France - called "Mother House".

The present Reverend Mother, Sister Joseph, next to a statue of Saint Mary Euphrasia — The Mother Foundress.

BRIEF HISTORY

The Good Shepherd Order of Nuns was founded by Saint Mary Euphrasia, who was a native of Normandy. There are convents of the Good Shepherd in the five continents of the world. The Mother House is in Angers, France. In 1848 Mother Euphrasia acceded to a request from a Miss Reddon in Limerick city. The invitation was timely and welcome because of the French Revolution that was then raging, and religious houses were the object of popular hatred. A foundation in Ireland offered a pied-a-terre in the event of forced exile from France.

The Sisters reached Limerick on the 18th February 1848. Throughout the years many convents were established: Waterford 1858, New Ross, County Wexford in 1860, Belfast in 1868, Sunday's Well, Cork 1870, Clifton, Cork in 1912, Derry, N. Ireland in 1919, Newry, N. Ireland in 1945, Dunboyne, County Meath in 1955 and Elingtron Road, Dublin in 1960.

The service of the Sisters in all these houses is directed towards children. Care, guidance and protection is their constant aim.

The author (right) with Mother Brendan (centre).

PREFACE

The events in this book are based on true facts. It is a tribute to the work and dedication of the Good Shepherd Nuns. Not only in Eire but in their many convents around the world.

The nuns cared for Frances for ten and a half years. She remembers their goodness, graciousness and generosity.

The First Mistress of that time achieved little success with her well-intentioned efforts to guide the young girl, whose feelings were tense and confused, and who demonstrated distress by resentment.

Chastisements demanded respect by force. Therefore a perpetual state of crisis prevailed between the First Mistress and her charge. The relationship was fraught with difficulties.

A bond had been formed over the first six years with a loving, kind but sick young mother and Frances. That bond was irrevocably broken by the death of her mother. No-one in authority could take her place. The First Mistress was in a vulnerable position. The highest grade of distinction, for meritorious action belongs to the many volunteers in Cork City, who work diligently and relentlessly to ease the burden of duties on the Good Shepherd Nuns, even to this day.

Frances was powerfully affected by the nuns who were her school teachers. Their attitudes and values and enthusiasm awakened in Frances a joy for learning, that buffered and neutralised her grief and hopelessness. They helped to build a foundation in self esteem, with praise and justice in her efforts and achievement.

INTRODUCTION

The Good Shepherd Convent was opened in May 1870. There was a great need at that time for some kind of school to care for, and to educate, a growing number of deprived and underprivileged children in Cork. Efforts were made to root out destitution which lay behind deprivation, and neglect by providing the deprived child with education, education for employment, which characterised the care of the late nineteenth century. Some children, in their need for compensation for an all too loveless life, were able to accept, and use this. Orphans too were in need of help. the Most Reverend Dr. Delaney, who was Bishop of Cork was very concerned about these children. In Mr. James Hegarty, who was the Lord Mayor of Cork, he found a sincere ally. Mr. Hegarty provided a large building and three acres surrounding it, to be used to house needy children. The Bishop wrote to the Good Shepherd Nuns for help. From Angers, France, the Mother General organised the transfer of four Irish nuns to Cork from Waterford, and one of them, namely St. Teresa Devereux, was appointed Mother Superior. The group of Sisters were met at Cork Station by the Mayor Mr. Hegarty, and some of the Clergy. Bishop Delaney and more of the priests waited for them at their temporary convent building, to give them a warm welcome. The Mayor's main concern was for the children, and within seven weeks a large building was erected to accommodate 90 children.

In May 1870 an orphan was admitted, and within three months 52   children were in residence.

There was a property of 5 acres adjacent to the Convent, and it was an ideal site for a permanent residence. The owner, Mr Kiely refused to sell, and the Nuns prayed to St. Joseph for help.

In a short time Mr. Kiely offered the land to the Nuns for a very moderate sum of £200. Mr. James Hegarty was devoted to helping the Nuns. He was filled with zeal and energy from the time he formed the project of a Convent in Cork. He collected money for building, and subsequent subscriptions, and many stories and anecdotes are told of his good humour when seeking donations. His friends called the orphanage Hegarty's Folly! During the years 1870 - 1950 the Sisters tried to be self-supporting. The lovely children excelled at needlework, crochet, and book-binding and won many prizes at book exhibitions. The Sisters also ran a commercial laundry to alleviate financial pressures. The Cork people have always responded magnificently, even to this day.

CHAPTER ONE

The morning was cold and damp on 28th October 1939. Pitch dark outside at 5 a.m. Granny was up and about. She had hardly slept that night, she was a tall and elegant lady for her 70 years. Her soft silver hair tied in a neat bun at the back of her head. Her face reflected the pain she carried in her heart. Her only daughter, age 32 years, had died of tuberculosis, after years of hopeful and bad times, with her health. Now the two grandchildren, Frances age 6 years and Kathleen age 8 years were to be taken from Granny and perhaps placed in a Convent School for orphans. There was one such place in Dublin City, only two miles away from Granny, but no doubt that place would be full, thought the old lady. So many men had gone to England to join the British Army or to the factories. Where mothers couldn't cope the authorities took the children into care. Granny lit a fire. She washed and dressed. Porridge for the children was routine, but this morning was special. The social worker, Mrs Clarke, would be there at 9 a.m. to take the children to court. Would their Father be at the hearing? Would he fight to keep them?

His sister, Aunt Mollie, loved the children and she was a good woman. She had two young sons and already a widow. The court would not add two little girls to her burden. Life in a Convent could be good, certainly the children would receive a good and useful education. Granny had heard that the Nuns could be very strict, maybe even cruel. She had spoken about the Convent to the girls, just in case, and she observed their reaction as she talked about having their own beds and beautiful toys to share and friends to play with. But, Kathleen was adamant "Don't let them put us in a school Granny, they'll kill us there." Frances was quiet and deep. She had always lived with Mother. They played and sang songs together and when mammy was often very ill, Frances would sit alone with her, bringing drinks and ever ready to run to Granny's with news.

Granny lived about half a mile away at Dorset Place in a little cottage. On this sad morning, Granny knew that once the children left the cottage she would never see them again. It was unlikely that Aunt Mollie would be given custody, so, they would go to a school. The distance to the Provincial schools was too far for her to visit them. there was one at Limerick, Waterford, Cork and Newry. All were at least 200 miles away from Dublin. Kathleen dressed in silence. Frances chatted merrily to keep Granny happy. Though two years younger than Kathleen she was much more sensitive to Granny's feelings. Other people's troubles affected her and for purely selfish reasons she would endeavour to lighten their burden by reassurance, a little song, or even absolute fibs, whatever worked best!

Mrs Malee, from No. 1, knocked to say goodbye to the children. She handed each a little bag of chocolate covered biscuits.

"Oh Granny, they'll be back to see us, as grand ladies, won't you Frances," said the kind neighbour. Frances nodded with a forced smile, although her young heart was breaking with despair, hearing Mrs

12

Malee's comment. With purpose the child spoke

"Mrs Malee, we'll be going to live with Aunt Mollie. She lives by the Phoenix Park, so I can see you and Granny whenever we like." Mrs Malee's face took on a serious look as she turned to Granny. "Did ye not tell them 'tis to the Convent they'll be goin', until they are sixteen or maybe more. 'Twill be grand an' all, a good education, yous will be grand ladies, and yous can go to America or anywhere, when yous are out." Frances took in every word. Kathleen sobbed and cried. Granny was crying too. Another knock on the door.

"That'll be Mary McCarthy to see the children," said Granny. Mary entered the cosy cottage and took a stool by the peat fire. She held up a holy medal on a string for each child. Mary hugged and kissed the children,

"Be good girls for the Nuns and don't forget us all, here in Dublin." Mary turned to Granny "The awl fella is up the lane, 'tis the 28th." Granny had forgotten the English man who collected the rent for the absentee landlord, who owned all the cottages in Dorset Place and lived in England. They never knew for sure whether the rent collector came over from England to collect rents, or if he lived in Dublin. None of that interested Granny that morning. She paid 2/6d per week. A lot of money from an old lady in 1939. A car pulled up alongside the cottage.

"Tis them," said Mrs Malee. Granny reached for the children's coats. Kathleen's crying grew louder. She pleaded with Granny to send the car away. Granny hugged them both, and gave each a little knitted doll, and held on to Kathleen as Mrs Malee opened the door. A long black car pulled alongside the cottage, the driver wore a uniform. Mrs Clarke struggled out of the front seat, she was a huge lady.

"Good morning, Mrs Reilly," she called to Granny, "are they ready?" she asked. The children were steered towards the kind social worker. Kathleen's screams, and tears, had little effect on Mrs Clarke. It was an every day drama in her thankless job.

"Say goodbye to Granny now, and sure you can send her lovely letters."

"Oh, dear God," said Granny, "will Mollie not get them?"

"Not at all, Mrs Reilly, hasn't she got two boys to bring up, and isn't she a widow." said Mrs Clarke pushing the children into the rear seat. "They've an Uncle Frank in Kildare, he's a major in the Irish Army, he might help," tried Granny.

"Now Mrs Reilly, listen to me, these little girls will be better off with the nuns. They'll learn well and be able to take their place in life as two Catholic girls. Their mother would like that. You are the best person to have them, but in ten years time you will be eighty and Frances will be only sixteen years old. Parting with them hurts you, but it is the best for the children that the court will send them to the nuns."

"Will they stay in Dublin?" asked Granny, hoping she could visit them.

"Depends, Mrs Reilly, on how many vacant places there are available."

"Maybe their father will be at the court and be able to help," said Granny, although in her heart she knew that he was a very selfish man who thought only of his own comfort. Mrs Clarke closed the car door to secure the children, she walked the few paces towards Granny.

"Mrs Reilly, I'll let you know where the children are sent. You must write to them. Even if their father comes to court I can tell you now that he has joined the British Army. That won't do him much good in our courts!"

Granny and her kind neighbours waved goodbye to the children, and the old lady knew that she would never see them again. The death of her only child had broken her heart. They had been so very close. Therese, she called her, although she was baptised Constance Therese.

Her daughter had married against her wishes - a dreamer. Writing poetry and walks in the Phoenix Park, with not a thought in his head about looking for a day's work, unless it was riding horses at the Curragh, in Kildare. Exercising horses and accompanying the race horse to England, to Cheltenham and Oxford. These trips only filled his head with further dreams and fantasies. He loved the English, and talked of them in glowing terms. Cheltenham was paradise to him. Most of the money earned in England he spent on fine clothes and the softest leather shoes, for himself. All travelling expenses paid by contract. He returned to Ireland dressed as an English gentleman. His wife was always happy to have him home. It was during her first pregnancy that her cough became tiresome.

Therese would laugh it off and say "'twas a cold, just gone, only the cough lingered." Kathleen was born at the Mater Hospital. She created washing and ironing and sleepless nights for an already sick mother. When Therese's husband returned to Cheltenham, she returned to her mother. Granny took over caring for the baby and encouraged her daughter to rest. With rest, fresh air and good food she seemed stronger. Then her husband returned home and over the next three years she had two miscarriages. Then Frances arrived safely. Granny kept Kathleen to relieve her daughter. Frances was a much easier baby; content, and Therese enjoyed strolls with her husband and baby through the beautiful walks in the Phoenix Park.

He would relate his experience among the English gentry in Cheltenham, and always had stories of the racing fraternity. It was during these weeks at home that he noticed his wife's coughing attacks were worse, and he encouraged his wife to see a doctor. When the money ran low he left for England, or to the Curragh. Racing the horses, early morning exercising them, stables to clean out, whatever was asked of him. He loved horses and lived near the stables in Kildare. In Dublin Therese visited St. Stephen's Hospital. The doctors told her that she had contracted tuberculosis. The disease that pursues relentlessly. Therese and her Mother had no one to help them. While the Granny kept Kathleen, Therese cared for Frances. There was no treatment other than slow death in an isolation hospital. The patient had not realised that her death was imminent. She hoped to see her children grow up, and then she would die peacefully, if a new cure did not come to patients with tuberculosis.

Over the following six years her husband worked from time to time between England and Kildare.

Therese moved to her Mother in his absence, and on his return she would join him at their small apartment in Parnell Street. It was one of Granny's neighbours, Mrs Malee, who alerted Granny to the usefulness of Mrs Clarke, the Social Worker. She helped on all cases of children in need. Granny was worried about her daughter's health. Mrs Malee arranged a visit for Therese to talk to Mrs Clarke. Frances who was five and a half years old sat by her mother and listened with interest to her worries. She was a bright child and soon realised that her mother would have to go into hospital. There was talk of the nuns to take care of the children. Frances looked at her mother for protection.

"No, Mrs Clarke, I'll stay with my children," said the sick mother. Frances worried daily and kept her fears to herself. She watched Granny feeding her weakened daughter with soup. Therese, gasping for breath. The cough was tiresome. One afternoon while Mrs Clarke was visiting, an ambulance arrived. Two men entered the cottage and picked up the young mother. She was so thin. Her long dark hair fell from her shoulders as they carried her outside. The children were allowed to say goodbye. Frances was shocked to see her taken away and wanted to cry, and scream, but Granny needed help. The child's mind was in turmoil. Mrs Clarke asked Granny for her son-in-law's address to keep him informed. Granny disliked her son-in-law. She considered him selfish, vain and irresponsible. She had never seen him demonstrate any affection for his children. "Make them and leave them" seemed to be his policy.

17

Some months later, unexpectedly Mrs Clarke arrived. Granny's tears upset the children and Mrs Clarke took Frances on her knee and told her that her mother could not come home. Kathleen cried bitterly. Frances found it difficult to believe that her mammy would not come home again. Mrs Clarke did not say that their mother was dead. Frances believed that one day soon her mammy would get better and come home. She would not cry, to cry was to accept bad news. Kathleen was crying, she was always crying. Frances would not say any night prayer with Granny that night. She feared prayers, they were never happy prayers. She wanted to laugh and to play and to see Granny smile again. Kathleen was such a whinger. Now, 28th October, Granny was crying. This time her grandchildren were being taken away.

CHAPTER TWO

People hurried to and fro on that cold October morning as the car sped on to the Children's Court. The driver, a family man, glanced in his mirror at the two little redheads in the rear.

"How old was their mother? he asked.

"Thirty two years old," answered Mrs Clarke.

"She must be in heaven," said the driver, as if to comfort the children. It was no comfort to Frances and she refused to accept it. As the car drew up by the main entrance Frances looked along the queue of people. She spotted Aunt Mollie and daddy. Uncle Frank was there too. They crowded by the car door to take the children. Mrs Clarke got very excited.

"no, no," she said to the relatives, "there are certain formalities to be done before the case, you will see them in court." Kathleen relaxed a little, encouraged by the sight of her relatives. The two children had never been close. they were brought up separately. Different in temperament and character. Kathleen was rather reserved, almost introvert. Frances was extrovert, a chatterbox but didn't like change or upheaval. Kathleen cared very little for her young sister. Frances would say or do anything for a quiet life. Pushing away the thought of her mother's death was easy. Stopping Kathleen from crying and sobbing called for fibs.

"If we go to a school it will be beautiful. There are dolls everywhere and friends to play with," encouraged the young sister. Kathleen quietened again and the children were led into a large room.

They were seated between Mrs Clarke and a uniformed man. The two adults spoke across the children in a whisper.

"The little one is grand, not a sound from her. Who knows what she is thinking," said the man to Mrs Clarke. They seemed to be waiting for someone to arrive and Mrs Clarke kept a watch on the big oak door. Pieces of paper were being handed around. Officials stared at the children, and whispered to each other. Suddenly, Kathleen yelled

"I'm not going to any school, they kill children there." Mrs Clarke tried to calm her charge and spoke quietly to her. The big doors opened. Frances caught a glimpse of Aunt Mollie in the hallway. All eyes were on the old gentleman with white hair who had just sat down on a lofty chair. All those who stood up when the old man entered, sat down again.

The kind old gentleman asked for the children's father to be brought in. Mr Donnelly entered the room with the grace and air of an English squire. He stood to the right of the Judge.

"You are the father of these two little girls?" the Judge asked.

"Correct," came the curt reply.

"You are no doubt aware that we have to decide their care and education here today. Their mother is not here and you have joined the British Army.

Mr Donnelly leaned forward and in a clear and firm voice he replied

"My sister, Mrs Hayes is here and she wishes to take them into her care. She is a good and capable woman. She lives at Parkgate Street. She is a widow, with two boys of her own, but I will help her financially."

"How does Mrs. Hayes support herself and the boys now?" asked the Judge.

"She works night shift in a laundry, but she has a friend, Dolly Murray, to sleep in the house." The Judge leaned back in his chair, holding a pencil between the thumb and forefinger of each hand.

"Mr Donnelly, these children, these two little girls, would benefit a great deal if we sent them to a Convent School until they are at least sixteen years old," advised Justice McCarthy. Mr. Donnelly gripped the back of the chair in front of him and leaned forward; he began in a determined but low key,

"Sir, these are my children, and if you take them away, you will break their spirit, as you would do to any young filly who is not treated with gentle handling. Religion is the opiate of this country ....." There the Judge stopped him, "Take this man outside," ordered an obviously angry Judge. He waited as Mr. Donnelly struggled with an attendant. Looking back at the Judge the obnoxious parent shouted,

"Let me take them to England, this Country is poisoned with religion." As his voice trailed off and the two little girls were crying and confused the Judge spoke to them.

"You will be very happy with the nuns in Cork. My sister is a nun at the Good Shepherd Convent and there you will have many children to make friends with." He turned to Mrs. Clarke and nodded his satisfaction.

Officials helped to escort the children from the Court. Kathleen was crying loudly. Frances was numb with grief. It was useless for Kathleen to cry and scream, Frances could see that.

"You'll see," Kathleen shouted through tears to Frances, the Nuns will kill us," and then she kicked at Mrs. Clarke and a helpful attendant.

"I want my Granny," screamed Kathleen. Frances was sick with shame. Her older sister crying and screaming, she could find no words, no fibs to shut her up. the corridor was crowded with all kinds of people, Mrs Clarke and her helper pushed the children along towards the street door. All the time ignoring everything that Kathleen did or said. The relatives were nowhere to be seen. Outside the driver opened the rear door of the waiting car. The little ones were shoved inside. Mrs Clarke took a seat beside them. They felt squashed, Mrs Clarke was such a big lady she took up most of the space.

"To the Station?" asked the driver, he obviously knew the routine. Mrs Clarke handed Kathleen a handkerchief. She accepted it, but cried even louder.

"Hush up there now," said the driver, "listen to me," he continued with his eyes on the road and on the traffic, "Now where yous is goin' is a great place. I wish I could go there. Wait'll you see the toys and everything, ah, sure yous will love it dare." His Dublin working class accent was familiar to them, and it had a warm and credible tone. Frances was resigned to give it a try, but she was grieving for her Mother, and felt sure she wasn't dead. Kathleen was so used to Granny, her feelings were for her kind and gentle Granny. The station came into view. The driver helped them out and held onto them while Mrs Clarke dragged her large body from the back seat.

She thanked the driver and she took each child by the hand. The children wouldn't have run away. They were well behaved little girls, just very upset at that sad time. The driver had another shot at reassuring them.

"It'll be like goin' on hollydays, ah, sure yous is goin' to love it dare, yous'll see I'm roight". Frances could see the tears in the kind man's eyes.

"Go on now with Mrs Clarke, and God bless ye both." His kindly disposition and gentle voice were reassuring to Frances. The station staff greeted Mrs Clarke. They knew her job was not an easy one.

"And who have we got for biscuits today," said the guard, looking at the children, "will yous let an auld man like me have some a dem courls," he said as he tousled Frances' red curly hair. He looked at Mrs Clarke, "is it to the Good Shepherds they're goin'? he asked in a sympathetic tone.

"'Tis," she answered, and she lifted each child up into the carriage.

"God bless them," said the old guard. Mrs Clarke opened a bag and brought out a flask and some sandwiches. The children refused any food. They were still holding Granny's dolls and the little bags of biscuits from Mrs. Malee. In a short while they were both asleep.

They slept on as the train journeyed to Cork City. They might as well sleep, thought Mrs Clarke. They were too young to appreciate the beautiful scenery. Mrs Clarke had made this journey so often. It was a busy time for all social workers. They had no official or professional training, just dedicated men and women motivated by a strong religious belief. World

War II had started, and many Irishmen left for England to join the army. The pressure on poor families worsened, and so did the pressure of work on social workers, as the need for schools such as The Good Shepherd Convent School was great indeed.

Cork City was close and Mrs Clarke woke the children. They looked about them curiously. Cork City was a bustling busy place.

The train stopped with a jerk, and Mrs Clarke stepped down. She lifted each child onto the platform and taking them by the hand she walked to the taxi rank.

"The Good Shepherd Convent, please," the children heard her say.

The driver gave the children a broad smile. He spoke to Mrs Clarke but the children could not understand his accent. It was too fast! and up and down! They reached the Convent in ten minutes. The taxi turned into the drive. It was dark outside. Up the long avenue they drove, and the Convent was lit up. There were three large buildings, all the lights were on. One light was so bright that Frances could see a big statue in the centre of the lawn. She didn't feel afraid, only interested and in wonder. She wanted to see the other children, the toys! Kathleen was crying again. The taxi stopped by a large oak door. there were several steps to the door. Mrs Clarke got out much easier that time. The taxi driver tried talking to the children again. His smile was nice but his words were almost foreign to the Dublin children. A nun approached them.

"Hello," she said softly, "come inside." The children alighted and the Nun took them by the hand.

"My name is Mother Sacred Heart," she said slowly and they mounted the steps. They reached the Hall, Mrs Clarke was handing some papers to another nun.

"The small one is Frances and the other one is Kathleen," said Mrs Clarke. Frances glanced up at their escort seeking reassurance or some final word of comfort. The social worker had already adopted a dispassionate stance. The child felt the pain of rejection and it registered profoundly. Without any delay Mother Sacred Heart took them to the inner hall. There Frances saw two more huge statues, one was of a nun.

Down the stony stairs, and into a room filled with clothes. Shelves on either side reaching the ceiling. There were two bigger girls in the room and the Nun introduced Frances and Kathleen.

"These two little girls are from Dublin. This is Frances and this is Kathleen," said Mother Sacred Heart.

"Hello," said one of the girls to Frances. "My name is Betty O'Donnell, and I have a sister Rita." Frances liked Betty and while the children were fitted with skirts and jumpers and underwear by the two bigger girls Mother Sacred Heart left them saying she wouldn't be too long. As soon as the nun disappeared Kathleen asked her most worrying question.

"Do the nuns kill children, or eat them?" Betty's face was a picture of shock, and the other girl, Mary Regan, assured Kathleen that the Nuns were very kind to good girls. Betty and Mary took them to a bathroom upstairs, and put both children into a bath of hot water. Washed and dried, the children were dressed in white nightdresses and taken up another flight of stairs to the top Dormitory. Mother Agnes was there to receive them. Betty promised Frances that she would see her after Mass the next morning. She explained to the bewildered child that she slept in a Dormitory down one flight of stairs, with older girls. Kathleen and Frances were shown their beds by Mother Agnes. This gentle and motherly nun assured them that they would be very happy.

"We don't talk in the dormitory," said the nun, "it is just a rule for all the children." Kathleen's bed was two rows away from Frances. Tucked up in bed Frances closed her eyes, but could not forget the scene in the court that morning. She wondered about Granny alone in her cottage. She wondered how long it would take to grow up, and then knock on Granny's door and see her Granny's smiling face! She could hear her sister Kathleen quietly crying. Peeping from the bedclothes Frances could see Mother Agnes, quietly walking up and down. Not a word was spoken by another child. They were all sleeping. The sheets felt cold and the pillow had a strange smell like hay or straw. The blanket was too low on her shoulder for any warmth, so the weary child snuggled down and became lost in a strange world. The first night of what was to become ten and a half years!

Early next morning the children were wakened by a bell in Mother Agnes's hand. Four or five times she rang a loud bell. Older girls were hurrying about encouraging little ones to "get up, come on, out of bed, get up." Frances and Kathleen hurried to the washroom where Mother Agnes gave each of them a clean towel and a toothbrush. Frances watched the routine and followed as quickly as she could. Mother Agnes dipped the toothbrush into a mug of salt, and Frances was amazed at the idea for cleaning her teeth! Another child approached Frances, and whispered

"What's your name?" Frances whispered her name with a smile. "My name is Rosanna, and don't talk until after Mass," advised Rosanna and Frances nodded in thanks. The children rushed about in various stages of dress. Four year olds had their hair brushed by ten year olds, all anxious to be ready at the next bell for Mass. Mattresses had to be turned and beds left to air. Little white veils were handed to each child to place on their heads and tied under their hair ready for church. Mass was 7.30 a.m. Another bell, children darted from all directions of the dormitory, washroom and lavatories to line up by the exit. Mother Agnes unlocked the dormitory door and the queue filed out in twos. Frances was partnered with Bunny Welsh. The children smiled at each other as Mother Agnes introduced them.

"You're the same age," said Mother Agnes. On down a long staircase and as it wound round Frances saw Betty O'Donnell at the head of another long line of girls in twos, they wore similar veils to the younger children from the top dormitory. Silence reigned everywhere. Mother Sacred Heart was standing near Betty, and as Frances glanced at the nun, Mother Sacred Heart responded with a warm smile. On down more stairs, right into a hall, that Frances remembered from her arrival, on through a long cloister, and into the Church. She kept close to Bunny and knelt alongside her. Lifting her chin as high as she could, enabled her to see over the handrail of her benchseat.

A small but beautiful altar on the children's side of the Church, with a wide ornate Communion rail for the children. Long wide oak bench seats and large stained glass windows in blue and red, greens and gold. The confession boxes were situated at the bottom end of their side of the Church, and a podium for the First Mistress, who attended Mass with the children every morning. The children filed up to the top benches, little ones first, and filled up the benches, all in place, to await the arrival of Father Aherne, the School Chaplain, and local Parish Priest. The beautiful church was built in 1870 in three sections. The nuns had the centre aisle with full view of the main altar.

The children's aisle had an altar to Our Lady of Perpetual Succour. The third aisle was for the laundry ladies etc. and honoured St. Joseph on that altar. In 1939 there were 82 children at the school, but as the 1940-1945 war advanced there were as many as 120. For the very young children the Mass dragged on.

Every morning in the Church, lowered heads on tiny hands were more likely to be sleepy tots than praying tots. The three bells at the Sanctus woke them with a startle. The distribution of Communion was an interesting event for any new child. Each Communicant would be well observed as she passed along the communion rail. Frances and Kathleen watched with keen interest. Red heads, dark curly heads, tall girls, short girls. It was difficult to notice eyes as they were generally cast downwards in reverence, with hands joined as in prayer. The Mass seemed to last forever. Frances was very hungry. The Mass was said in Latin, and then the Priest recited a special prayer for an end to the war. The prayer was in English, Frances soon realised as days went by that it signalled an end to Mass, and she looked forward to that prayer. When the service ended, the children left from the top end, in twos, and filed on down the aisle, hands joined as in prayer, and on to the outside corridor that led down to the Refectory, and breakfast. The First Mistress lingered, until the last couple of children filed out. All in absolute silence, to the Refectory's locked door. The First Mistress unlocked the door and the children took up their places on long benches by oil cloth covered tables. They waited for permission to 'sit'. A small brass bell, shaped as a crinoline lady, in the land of the Nun signalled for grace, and then permission to sit and eat.

Each place was set with a tin mug, tin plate and a porridge spoon at breakfast time. A large plate in the centre of the table held slices of bread already buttered, enough to give each child two slices. A senior girl attended each table and served a watery type of porridge called gruel. She filled each mug with warm milk. Milky skins floated on the surface. That was routine breakfast. If the First Mistress felt inclined, she would give permission to the children to talk to each other. She signalled with a ring on the tiny bell she carried in her pocket. Immediately she touched the bell the Refectory became alive with chatter. Voices exploded in loud chatter, and laughter and clanging of tin mugs. The release of pent up feelings and the expression of freedom to talk was deafening and certainly frightening for any newcomer!

Frances and Kathleen were plagued with questions. They were seated at different tables, according to age. As the years rolled by close friends were more important than any sisterly bond. The new children were asked their names, where did they come from; was their Mother dead; was there any chance of a gift parcel from relatives; until Frances gave in to tears. The nun quickly observed the situation and approached the child.

"Eat your bread, and drink your milk," suggested Mother Sacred Heart.

"I don't like the skins," cried Frances.

"They are good for you," the Mistress encouraged.

"I want to go home and I hate that stuff, the skins and the lumps are terrible and . . ." The children started laughing and said that Frances had a funny accent.

"Get on with your breakfast," said the patient nun in a soft tone. "This little girl has a Dublin accent and it will soon change," continued their nun.

The time was up, breakfast was over, and a touch on the bell brought instant silence. The noise of moving benches on the tiled floor and the clatter of tinware being collected, and the awful sight of breadcrumbs and milk spillings made Frances pleased to get out of the Refectory. Still hungry she moved off with the children, to the dormitory, to tidy the beds before schoolwork. She was learning the daily routine.

Following other children, she climbed the stairs called the Visitors Stairs, because it was the quickest route to both dormitories. The children, in general, didn't understand why it was called the Visitors Stairs. No visitors ever walked there! It was a magnificent oak stairway, very wide, and wound about, and up, reaching four floors. The balustrade was highly polished and the rungs were turned by real craftsmen, in the late 19th Century. On and up four flights of stairs, past the door that led to the lower dormitory, and on up to the top dormitory, to make beds, clean sinks and sweep floors. Many hands made light work! A final washing of hands, hair combed, then lined up in two in readiness for the school bell. Bed making for Frances on her first day was made easier by the help she received when Betty O'Donnell arrived to teach her. Betty was assigned to take charge of Frances.

Frances learned much from Betty. She learned that her number was 39, and that Betty would mark all her clothes with that number. Kathleen was given 72. All their days at Sunday's Well they would use those numbers to identify their property including shoes and sandals. Betty's responsibility was to keep an eye on Frances, to see that she kept herself clean and tidy until she could fend for herself. Now it was time to go to her first Teacher, Mother Clotilde. Betty placed her in line with the First class group. She stood with Bunny, Rosanna, Mary Laney, Rita, Mary Crumlin, Mary McDonoghue, Breda McCabe, Mary Mulvey, Noreen Hennessy, Cassie Hyde and many more five to seven year olds.

CHAPTER THREE

The school bell sounded and off went the children in their usual twos to the classrooms on the second floor. Frances was pleased with her enormous classroom. A large bright room with colour pictures on the walls. Mother Clotilde taught the five to seven year olds. The nun warmly welcomed her new pupil.

"Come to my desk," she invited Frances. "Now tell me your name and your age."

"My name is Frances Donnelly and I'm five."

"Can you count for me," said the teacher.

"Yes, one two three four five six seven eight nine ten eleven .....," boasted Frances.

"Alright, thank you," said a pleased teacher. Mother Clotilde opened up a chart with pictures and letters. The chart was made of cloth and had a wooden holder at each end with a cord to hang it if necessary. The teacher pointed to letters at random and was very pleased with her assessment so far. Forming letters with tiny sticks of various colours was the next task. Frances enjoyed it all very much. Then the nun brought some plasticine called 'marla', and asked the child to make anything she liked. Frances set about making a cottage, with a high wall all round. It had windows and a door with a knocker. Frances pinched out the top of the wall to represent broken glass pieces, as she had seen on her walks in Dublin. Mother Clotilde was very pleased with her attempt, and especially pleased with the idea of glass along the wall top. Frances explained that it was to keep bad people out. Mother Clotilde was so pleased that she showed the creation to the class and remarked how good it was. She also told the children that Frances came from Dublin and so did Mother Clotilde. Frances felt that she had a good friend and a good teacher. She felt secure with Mother Clotilde.

During the early years with her sick mother, Frances learned to read, to count and to form letters. In the Convent classroom with Mother Clotilde there were many occasions, when the child felt thankful for the help given to her by her own mother, during the good days they enjoyed together in Dublin. Thoughts of her mother were painful indeed.

The children did painting, cutting out, and forming pictures. Boxes of coloured paper lay neatly in cupboards. Tiny scissors and bottles of glue for sensible little girls were available, and coloured pencils and chalks all helped to make afternoons very happy ones. For many small children the mornings were spent learning the alphabet, counting and reading. Mother Clotilde was a dedicated teacher and no time was wasted. She was a wonderful storyteller. A sad one, a holy one, a ghostie one, whatever the choice, Mother Clotilde obliged and the children sat with chins cupped in tiny hands listening to her every word and were desperately sorry when the story ended.

The school day was from 9 a.m. to 3.30 p.m. A break for collation, then arts and crafts, cookery or laundry. Children were allocated yearly into various classes. Cookery and laundry classes took children from age 12 years upwards. Age groups were always kept together no matter how good or bad the child's ability. Monday to Friday were school days. Saturdays were house cleaning days, including gardening. At the age of 14 to 15 years a girl could sit for the Primary Leaving Certificate, then in her final year she would be allocated to some form of employment within the School or Convent until she was old enough, and responsible enough, to leave the nuns.

The school had six classes. The rooms were very large. Windows faced onto the school grounds and were very large sash types. Ceilings were lofty and Victorian. No central heating, and winter days were cold indeed. Floors were of hard wood and highly polished. Walls were painted, dark green half way then cream to the ceiling. Rather clinical in atmosphere. Huge sliding half glazed doors could divide off an extremely long room into three large rooms. These rooms were extra to Mother Clotilde's first classroom, and extra to the 5th classroom that housed the 6th year exam class. Each classroom was furnished with strong oak desks and chairs in neat rows and placed conveniently around a large blackboard and easel. Cupboards, well stocked with text books, pens, ink, pencils, rubbers, rulers, writing exercise books, maps and globes, all created an atmosphere to stimulate any pupil.

In each class, stock control was the responsibility of two girls - a well sought after task! Education was controlled by the Cork City Authority and their Inspector, a Mr. Hegarty, could walk in at any time and observe standards. Irish Language was compulsory and was part of the School Leaving Certificate.

Frances enjoyed school hours with Mother Clotilde and affectionately called her "Tilly", but never addressed the nun as such, just among the children.

Drill was compulsory every morning. Hoops and loops and dumb-bells were used in turn, to make each exercise interesting. The exercises also helped to warm the small children before the school work commenced. Tilly sang along with the children during the exercises. Frances enjoyed drill.

"Arms above your heads, up on toes and down, and again, ordered Tilly, and when everyone could follow the exercise in unison Tilly sang out the appropriate tune. It was great fun.

Mother Clotilde had a brother in Dublin, his name was Father Mac. Whenever he visited his sister the children too would enjoy a visit from him. Christmas was drawing near and Frances was nearly six weeks at the school when the Christmas decorations were brought out of storage. The older girls held the ladder while Mother Sacred heart decorated the classrooms. The colours were very pretty. Beautiful net curtains dressed the windows and gave a much homelier atmosphere. In class, colourful paper chains were made long enough to reach across the ceiling, corner to centre. Pretty twist patterns to decorate the tops of the pictures. For hours eager little fingers would link and stick coloured loops. The crib figurines were brought out of storage and washed ready for display. 16th December was the date every year to put up the crib. Suggestions for any new type of decoration was given fair consideration by "Tilly". The children worked like little beavers in silence while "Tilly" told the most wonderful Christmas stories.

On Frances's first Christmas she joined other children around a blackboard
to copy down a Christmas letter, to granny, and she used a pen and ink. All the children wrote the same letter, glancing at each word on the blackboard. With blotting paper held conveniently, to avoid "Blots". "Dear Granny, I wish you a happy and holy Christmas.........." The First Mistress collected up the children's letters and there the contact between Frances and Granny ended.

Christmas arrived and apart from each child receiving twelve sweets and a piece of cake at tea time from the nuns, in an environment of music and colourful decorations, no presents or cards or letters were ever received by Frances or Kathleen. Luckier children received dolls and teddies and were shared eventually by all the little ones. Money was never handed out, but the recipient was informed by the Second Mistress and in due course could spend it at the tuck shop whenever it was open. Sharing tuck with other children was not allowed, in some cases permission would be granted. The idea was to prevent any young bully from exploiting the owner. Frances was ever hopeful for a letter from Granny. Aunt Mollie didn't write either. Frances watched the First Mistress anxiously for a letter but with no luck, or so it seemed then. Sometime in 1940, Mother Sacred Heart disappeared, and the children were devastated. Frances felt very insecure. Mother Sacred Heart had played a great part in helping Frances to settle in. She was an approachable Nun. The children could talk to her, ask questions and they felt safe with her. Various ideas and suggestions about the nun's absence spread like wildfire through the school ranks. Wild imaginings led to all kinds of fear and resentment.

In a day it became clear that Mother Therese was promoted to First Mistress. Mother Lelia to Second Mistress. Almost at once Mother Therese became very strict. The children found her less easy to talk to. Frances avoided her whenever she could. That July the classes changed, but Frances remained with Mother Clotilde until July 1941. She was sad to leave "Tilly", and had been so happy in her class and had learned a great deal from that lovely Nun from Dublin. Months had gone by and Frances fitted into her peer group, and learned much in association, to give and to receive. To quarrel and make up. To discover the importance of standing up for herself among many children, with varying limits in tolerance, she soon learned not to be too assertive!

The move up to Mother Finbarr's class with Breda, Rosanna, Bunny, Mary and Mary Mulvey meant a great bunch were moving up. Mother Finbarr was quite strict and wanted very child to become expert with pen and ink and not a single blot was tolerated. Her second choice for her girls was for all of them to speak and read Gaelic. She worked relentlessly to achieve her goal. Frances learned Gaelic grammar and a wide vocabulary. She enjoyed the new language, as did most of her colleagues. Songs in Gaelic, and stories in Gaelic and Gaelic conversation brought the joy of achievement, to an otherwise disadvantaged group of children. Mother Finbarr was a patient teacher. She had a keen sense of humour when the mood took her! and much laughter was heard from Class 2. She brought relief from the tedium of classwork by teaching the children little drama scenes, involving pretty Gaelic songs. Mother Finbarr was also deeply proud of her religious name, and took time and effort to teach her class the life story of St. Finbarr, who was a Patron Saint of Cork, as well as of their school. The 25th September was her Feast Day and a school holiday was declared every year on that day. Mass on the morning of St. Finbarr's Feast Day was followed by a beautiful hymn to their Patron Saint sung by all the children from 2nd Class to senior girls, in Gaelic. "Caeg molah go heag le Naoive Corcaig" the children sang with enthusiasm and pride. Frances mixed well and established roots, giving her a secure feeling, and deep friendships were forming. Small tasks allocated by Mother Finbarr, e.g. distributing the lesson books, cleaning the blackboard, or filling up the ink wells gave her confidence, and a feeling that she was reliable and appreciated.

Stimulated by these feelings she developed a sense of belonging, and learned all that she could grasp from Mother Finbarr. Writing well, reading aloud clearly, spelling, tables and addition, subtraction and multiplication made for busy and enjoyable school hours. Mother Finbarr was generous in praise for Frances's classwork. That praise compensated for some very black looks that Frances noticed all too often, from the First Mistress - Mother Thérèse!

Children with varied personalities and abilities created a most competitive situation. Breda had a high academic ability and although Frances and Breda were always on good terms with each other,

Breda exercised caution reference their friendship in the presence of Mother Thérèse. Unlike Rosanna and Bunny who were brave friends. However, Frances gained in experience, with any "fair- weather friend" and she coped with their lack of loyalty.

Bunny was a nervous child. Her father was dead and her mother found caring for Bunny and her lovely sister Joan impossible, as she had to work in order to exist. There was no unemployment benefit or any hope of financial aid. Their mother went to England to work after seeking the help of the nuns to care for Bunny and Joan. She hoped that the situation would not last too long, anxious that her family would be united as soon as possible. However, year after year the children remained with the nuns. Bunny was extremely sensitive, the slightest remark by any child or teacher resulted in hours of tears. Frances reassured Bunny that life would improve and together they would chat and plan, this comforted Bunny and pleased Frances.

A very popular nun was chosen to prepare twenty 7 to 8 year olds for First Communion and Frances was delighted to learn that Bunny and Rosanna were in the First communion Class with her. Saturday mornings instruction was routine in the early months, and as the great day drew nearer the children attended extra sessions on two evening a week. Mother Teresa used magnificent picture books, and text books, to prepare the youngsters for their first Confession. Small fingers moved over the beautiful books, as if touching the heavenly figures and faces would somehow bring the pictures to life. They listened attentively as their gentle teacher told them stores of Jesus's life on earth. Frances listened with keen interest, and plagued the teacher with questions. Mother Teresa would always find a beautiful picture to illustrate a point.

"But, Mother," said Frances, "if the Communion Host is the flesh and blood of Jesus, why does it not pour blood when the Priest breaks it?" Mother Teresa always found a suitable answer, even if it rested on a promise to answer that "good question" next lesson!

The closer the children's first Confession neared, the more Frances worried about the sins they had to confess. Frances and Bunny walked together in the playground and discussed their sins.

"What will you tell," asked Bunny, "disobedience?" Frances deeply considered that sin, and it seemed very serious and quite bad, even if it was a venial sin.

"Did you ever tell lies?" asked Bunny.

"No!" lied Frances. Then as Frances looked through the Catechism book, she made her decision.

"Hey, Bunny, this is it," she exclaimed in whispered excitement, "you do the Fifth and I'll do the Sixth," encouraged Frances.

"But I haven't got anyone to kill," said Bunny.

"Well, that makes it alright. Remember Mother Teresa said to us, 'For example, say you killed your brother,' and then she added that it was no harm, as you had no brother!"

"Oh yes," said Bunny, looking quite satisfied, "you're right Frances, I have no brother, so I'll give an example."

"Good," replied Frances, "and I'll say I committed adultery. Mother Teresa told us that no-one bothers about that one, remember when she was teaching us she skipped over the Sixth." The young friends were very satisfied that they had sorted out their sins and looked forward to their first Confession.

The first Communion Day was one to remember. Even Mother Thérèse was in good form, as she hung a beautiful medal and a white cord around each child's neck. "Souvenir of my First Holy Communion" were the words on the reverse side of each medal. Then all twenty First Communion children walked in twos, to fill the front benches on each side of the children's section in church. Frances felt very grand in her white silk dress, beautiful veil and white shoes and socks. At communion during the Mass, the new participants led the line of Communicants to the altar. A very special ceremony in their lives, to remember always. As they received their Communion the choir of children sang for them:

"Jesus, thou art coming
Holy as thou art.
Thou the God who made me
To my little heart.
Jesus, I believe it, on thy only word
Kneeling I adore thee,
As my King and Lord.

Oh, what gifts or presents
Jesus can I bring
I have nothing worthy
Of my God and King.
But thou art my Shepherd,
I thy little lamb
Take my heart and fill it,
All I have and am.

Jesus Lord, I love thee
With my whole, whole heart
Not for what thou giveth,
But for what thou art.
Come, oh come, sweet Saviour
Come to me and stay.
For I love thee, Jesus
More than I can say."

Here, in their benches all dressed in white, on what was a very special day in the life of a Catholic child, knelt twenty very happy children and Mother Teresa, who prepared them for this lovely day, proudly observing each one of them from her position, that special morning in the children's bench.

After a very special breakfast, during which many of the Convent's nuns visited them, photographs were taken in groups, and individually. The day was indeed a happy one, and indelibly marked in the mind of each child.

CHAPTER FOUR

In September 1942 Frances went up to a new class, the Third Class and her new teacher was Mother Brendan, a Kerry Nun. The children loved Mother Brendan and Frances enjoyed to hear the story of Mother Brendan's day of decision to become a Good Shepherd Nun. This teacher explained to her new class that many years previously, during the "troubles" of Ireland, 1916-1921, her fiancé was mortally wounded. Mother Brendan and he were to have been married, and she helped the Irish soldiers with tea and nursing aid whenever she could. One day she was injured badly. While lying in hospital in great pain she promised "Our Lady" that if she recovered she would join the Good Shepherd Nuns and care for children.

Life in Mother Brendan's class was exciting, not a moment was wasted. Arithmetic was made fun to learn, with little anecdotes to help the memory. Reading in English was advanced, and in essays Mother Brendan looked for "splendid" words to enhance vocabulary. Beautiful poems she taught her children, and encouraged good diction. She would demonstrate to the class a recitation, with emphasis on word endings:

"The wonderful world is over me
And the wonderful wind
Is shaking the tree.
It walks on the water,
And whirls the mills,

And talks to itself
On top of the hills."

Mother Brendan was very pleased that she was a relative of Dennis O'Dea, the actor and she told simple but romantic stories of her life as a young girl. Her Feast Day was celebrated on 16th May and her natural love of entertainment would be demonstrated by taking her class to "The Hill" for a lovely picnic of scones and rhubarb jam and lemonade. The class would sing songs and Mother Brendan would recite one of her favourite poems:

"'He will not come,'
said the gentle child
As she patted the poor dog's head
And she pleasantly called him
And fondly smiled
But he heeded her not
In his anguish wild
Nor arose from his lonely bed.

'Twas his Master's grave
That he chose to rest.
He guarded it night and day
For a friend who had loved
And often caressed
Might never fade away."

Poetry was the nun's first love, and very often she would teach her children a little rhyme to illustrate a moral of a lesson:

"There's a neat little clock
In the centre it stands
And it points out the hour,
With its two pretty hands.
One points to the minute,
The other points the hour
As often you'll see
In the High Church Tower.

So must I, like the clock,
Keep my face happy and bright.
My hands when they move
They must always do right.
My tongue must be guarded
To say what is true
Wherever I go
Or whatever I do."

and at another time she wrote on the blackboard:

"The nicest words to use are these
Excuse me, thank you, if you please.
Such little Christian words are right
And liked by all because polite."

History became alive in Mother Brendan's class.
She was a sincere Nationalist. Children learned from
this wonderful teacher the difference between a real
love for Ireland and the danger of bigotry. Every
lesson was made enjoyable and Mother Brendan had
the gift of making each child feel an important
member of a team.

Before Frances moved on to the Fourth Class she

developed a painful inner left ear. It had developed over a few days. She had so far managed to avoid Mother Thérèse, but now she had to report the painful ear, as was the rule in any sickness or injury.

Passing along to breakfast one morning, she stopped in front of the First Mistress and said,

"Excuse me Mother, this ear is very painful". Instantly, the hand of the nun struck her hard across the sore ear. The pain sent the little girl reeling to the floor.

"How dare you give me this trouble," said the First Mistress. Frances, though astounded, was thankful. The painful throbbing ceased. Pus and discharge poured from her ear. Frances continued to breakfast holding her ear cupped in her small hand, and glancing back at Mother Thérèse she observed the nun cuddling affectionately her "pet lamb", Elsie Hackett. Children's natural keen sense of justice dealt with poor Elsie on many occasions. Elsie had the gift of a heavenly voice. Mother Thérèse's love of music cemented a special bond between the nun and that child.

Reverend Mother's Feast Day was celebrated on 24th April each year. For many weeks prior to that date the children rehearsed a play to perform for Reverend Mother, all the nuns and some guests. Mother Thérèse was Producer, Director, Choreographer and Stage Manager. She had a brilliant mind in the entertainment field. A gifted pianist and a lovely voice. Her face lit up at the piano. She adopted a warm and friendly attitude to everyone, but away from the entertainment atmosphere she became sour and serious. Most of the children were very sensitive to her mood swings and to protect herself Frances kept a safe distance. Slowly, the resentment Frances harboured, was seen by the First Mistress as sullenness towards her and, in an unprofessional manner, retaliated by humiliating and punishing her charge.

The evening before the performance, and although Frances had a part in the Butterfly Dance, the chatterbox child was seen talking on her way to the dormitory. She and her companion were reported to the First Mistress by a senior girl. Rosanna was spoken to severely and Frances was forbidden to see or take part in the performance the following evening. She was sent to the dormitory half an hour before the play started. All that day she had rallied around carrying costumes to and from the sewing room, all the time hoping for a reprieve, to no avail!

That night the music resounded throughout the school. Frances knew all the songs and she sang along with the music. She retreated to the sanctuary of the lavatory where the floor was tiled, and she danced the "Japanese Girls Dance". Visualising her young friends dancing in the performance, dressed in Kimonos and with their hair decorated either side with yellow chrysanthemums, they held pretty fans while they sang:

"Good evening we're gay little maidens
We are gay little girls Japanese
We have come from a beautiful country
Far over the blue sunny seas
We hope that you think we are pretty
Our eyes are quite lovely you see

We'll show you tonight if you listen
What a merry merry band are we
Gay little Japanese, gay little girls
    from Japan
Where no-one can do as they please
And everyone carries a fan.
Gay little Japanese maidens, gay little
    girls from Japan.

Our king is a dreadful Mecado
When he's cross he chops off our head
So we always must do as he tells us
'Cause we don't think it's nice to be
    dead.
But when we grow up and are bigger
We always will do as we please
Then we won't mind the dreadful Mecado
When we are quite tall Japanese.
    ...."

Eventually boredom set in and Frances felt quite
sorry for herself. Rosanna was talking to her
yesterday, yet she was downstairs enjoying the
performance. All things considered she decided to
interrupt the peaceful evening for the audience
below. The long dormitories and toilets were
situated directly above the classrooms and the
stage. Going from one lavatory to the other she
continued to flush each lavatory with a vengeance
and to slam each door in turn. A senior girl arrived
to investigage the noise and fairly explained to a
vindictive, attention-seeking child that in creating
such trouble she was investing in further

punishment. The play ran for a further night and Frances was sent upstairs again.

The first hour was quite interesting as she viewed the distant scenery from the large dormitory windows. The red bricked 19th Century school was situated high on a hill, overlooking the "Mardyke" lit up at night. The Bon Secuer Hospital was clearly seen, and Frances thought of Mother Teresa who had prepared her for her First Communion, and then had her operation at the "Bon Secuers". Then the horizon held the child's imagination. Dublin must be the other side of the horizon and Aunt Mollie could be waiting there, and Granny. They had promised to write letters but Mother Thérèse never seemed to have anything for her. She wondered if Mother Thérèse would still be angry the next morning, and with this thought Frances closed the lower dormitory door and mounted the stairs to her own dormitory.

Next morning she noticed a cold attitude from the other children.

"We are not to speak to you," said Pet Lamb Elsie Hackett. "You will have to apologise to Mother Thérèse. You will have to kneel in front of her in the refectory and we will all watch you, and you will have to say that you are sorry for giving trouble. She might forgive you, or she might not," continued Elsie, with a smug grin on her large mouth.

All through the day a busy routine kept Frances's mind at peace. Supper time came and she was ignored by all, her stubborn defiance surfaced. Eating her two slices of bread and margarine, and drinking her cocoa with an air of "who cares about you lot anyway" Frances got through that meal.

From time to time her eyes met those of Mother Thérèse. She was willing to say "sorry" but not until the following day, just to show Elsie Hackett how little she cared for Elsie's ideas.

After supper, as the children filed out of the refectory, the First Mistress took Frances aside. The cold stares from the other children allied with the nun only served to bring out the worst in the child. When the nun and the child had the privacy of an empty room Mother Thérèse spoke quietly and firmly,

"You are going to change your ways or I will beat you to within an inch of your life." This phrase Frances was to hear for some years to follow. "God gave you a good brain and you could be the best if you wanted to be," said the schoolmistress, and with a closed fist she knocked on the child's forehead with white knuckles while she warned, "I will be obeyed and you will pay respect, my lady". Frances backed to the door, and with tightly closed lips and a defiant expression, that showed a deliberate refusal to co-operate, she left the room.

Out of the nun's presence Frances raced off to her dormitory where Mother Agnes listened sympathetically to her problems.

"Don't talk in the ranks," advised the dormitory nun and confidante. "I know you are a good girl but you are a chatterbox and Mother Thérèse can be very angry. Wash and go to bed, and apologise tomorrow."

The drama of making the apology was traumatic. Frances was not sorry for any trouble she caused to Mother Thérèse and it was simply a charade to apologise. She just had to do it to satisfy Bunny and

Rosanna, so that they could talk together at playtime.

Lunchtime arrived. A space was made by her friends to help the grand entrance, to walk up the centre of the refectory, to kneel down and say that she was sorry for giving trouble. The nun stood beside her predium with arms folded under her gamp.

"I cannot hear you," she said in a scoffing tone. Frances repeated the words a little louder. Silence fell on all, as the nun considered the apology. Then in a loud and angry tone she answered the penitent.

"You arrived here with your sister because there was no-one to look after you when your mother died. Your father enjoys himself in England and recently your Grandmother died. I remember the night you arrived, so dirty we had to give you a bath," the Mistress paused to let her words take effect, then continued, "one can always tell the children who were used to better things. Your dead mother is looking down on you and I hope you will let her see a improvement in the future." With those words she left the refectory and Frances rose to her feet. If only she could run away. She could feel the eyes of every child upon her and piercing through her very soul. How could she ever lift her head up again. She walked to her table. Passing her sister Kathleen who was sobbing quietly, not only ashamed of her young sisters' behaviour and pained by Mother Thérèse's hurtful comments, but at the sad and sudden and cruel way they received the news of their Granny's death! Frances cried as if her heart would break and vowed to make Mother Thérèse pay for her words.

Mother Brendan soon heard the gossip of Frances's apology and found time to talk to her about the trouble. Frances related Mother Thérèse's words and Mother Brendan reassured her that the best way to win the war was to do well, "do better than Elsie!" said Mother Brendan "and remember that God loves you more when you suffer injustice". Mother Brendan told Frances that she was now good enough in class to move up to Fourth Class, to Mother Bridget. Leaving Mother Brendan's class was very sad indeed. No-one ever wanted to leave that wonderful human being, an understanding, dedicated teacher who loved her work for children.

CHAPTER FIVE

Mother Bridget was eccentric, of that there was no doubt. The children adored her. "Doodle-allie" the children called her. She would ramble on for an hour or more about the Battle of Clontarf 1014 A.D. She became very excited and confused and talked of how she made the tea with the ladies in Cum na man in 1014 A.D.!!, and knitted dark green helmets for the soldiers.

The class would choke and drown fits of laughing behind their reading books, she was confused with the Rising of 1916! Mother Bridget loved to hear the Gaelic language although she had forgotten it during her young years, when it was unwise to speak it. Her lovely face would light up at the sound of the Gaelic language being spoken by any child. In a more lucid moment she would ask

"Are you talking back there?" and Frances would reply

"No, Mother, I am teaching Bunny our Gaelic language." That answer always saved the day. The children puzzled about this nun. How could Reverend Mother not see that Bridget was doodle-allie? Every day was fun, very little was learned. Brian Boru and the Battle of Clontarf was all she ever wanted to discuss. The unreliable French Army were always too late with help. Clare and Limerick and Brian Boru, cum na man, the Black and Tans and De Valera, the year was absolute fun!

Mother Bridget was a favourite with the children and they respected her. They played little tricks for their own amusement, but if an Inspector came along they would put on an excellent show in work and attention, to support Mother Bridget. For all her ramblings this dear old nun would oblige with poetry, a gift she was blessed with. Most of the songs, concerts, for Feast Days and Jubilees were written and composed by Mother Bridget. She then set the words to the music using old Irish Ballads. On one occasion when the Mother Provincial made a visit to Cork from Anger, France the children greeted their V.I.P. in concert with one of Mother Bridget's songs:

"St. Finbarr's children
Greet you with song
Hail you Mother Provincial dear.
Gladly our voices
The strains prolong
Happy to have you here.

It is our delight,
To greet you tonight
Welcome, thrice welcome, from all.
Many a burden we know you bear
Even though your face
Wears oft a smile
Happy we'd be if our earnest prayer
Would lighten them all the while."

The children loved to entertain, and enjoyed verse speaking, poetry, Irish dancing, drill, singing solo and choir. Mother Bridget took a keen interest. The costumes were made by the senior girls under the guidance of Mother Lelia.

Mother Bridget had a particular phobia about the care of text books being kept in perfect condition. She delegated the task of checking all books, to two girls, every Saturday for wear or tear. A list of owners of torn books was placed on her desk for Monday morning. Mother Bridget read the riot act to any culprit and the children knew the Nun's weakness for rambling, and would draw on this to confuse the teacher, by asking questions about St. Patrick and St. Columcille and the Book of Kells, she would suddenly look at her watch and make a move towards the door! Children would rush to open the door for her and hope that their kindly "doodle-allie" teacher would forget to return to the classroom.

During the Fourth Year, Domestic Science, and senior level Arts and Crafts became part of the school schedule. Each day at 3.30 groups made their way to those classes. Frances enjoyed learning to knit, to sew and to use a sewing machine. Crochet and embroidery, cooking and laundering and ironing.

The Cookery Room was a long airy room that opened onto a courtyard. Tables were arranged in rows, one behind the other where one or two pupils would work to each table. There was only one cooker, a gas model, and somehow the young cooks never felt under stress for cooking space. Omelettes and sauces, to whole dinner courses and desserts and pastries, filled two hours for each group of 12 - 15 year olds every evening.

Mother Bridget was not involved in teaching any of these subjects. Mother Clotilde taught knitting, sewing, embroidery and crochet. Mother Stanislaus taught cookery. Frances disliked cookery, she found the subject too slow, but had an interest in housewifery. Pots and pans she made sparkle and sinks thoroughly cleaned. She volunteered to "wash up" for her colleagues to escape cooking. Mother Stanislaus taught Frances to make a white sauce. Frances made no secret of the fact that she would be happier with two hours of history. Cookery exams were a yearly event. Mother Stanislaus was an excellent teacher, and very patient. A most approachable teacher, she related very well to her young students.

When Frances was twelve years old she prepared for her first cookery exam. The candidates were all dressed in white overalls and white headscarves. The Examiner walked slowly along the tables, giving each girl a dish to prepare and cook. Frances watched Mother Stanislaus for encouragement as the Examiner drew near. On her table was a bowl with three eggs. The Examiner smiled and invited the child to separate the three eggs. Frances froze, and placed each egg approximately six inches apart, then looked up with confidence. "Is that how you separate eggs?" the Examiner asked in amazement. Frances glanced at her teacher and the expression on the nun's face proved that the student was in deep trouble. The Examiner continued questioning, "What are you going to do when you grow up and go into the world if you cannot separate an egg?" Frances felt no shame. She disliked food preparation and cooking. She made no reply. The Examiner moved away and Mother Stanislaus was obviously disappointed. At that time in her life food was cooked for Frances and she had little guarantee of ever growing up at the rate Mother Thérèse used the strap or cane! Frances moved to the scullery and washed pans and gave as much help as she possibly could. Invariably Mother Stanislaus popped in with another pot or pan and hurried away again to keep an interest in her cook's efforts. Eventually all dishes were put on display. The meat by Mary, cabbage by Breda, mashed potatoes creamed by Noreen, stewed rhubarb and custard by Pauline and Bunny, rock cakes by Joan and scones by Sheila.

All the girls were flushed and excited. The Examiner checked all pots and pans, angles and handles, cupboards and shelves and drawers of cutlery. "One hundred percent" for cleanliness brought a happy smile to Frances's face. "Well," said the Lady Examiner, "you may not have much interest in cookery, but you can try your hand as a scullery maid." With a friendly smile she bade farewell to the class and encouraged the children to eat the food so nicely prepared and cooked.

No sooner had she left the room when in walked Mother Thérèse. Mother Stanislaus who was happy and cheerful and in a playful mood remarked to the First Mistress that Frances Donnelly could not separate three eggs, and disclosed the method Frances had used. Mother Thérèse approached the table and ordered the child to separate the same eggs. Frances obeyed at once and separated the yolk from the white in no time. Mother Stanislaus was amazed.

"Why did you not do that for your exam?" she asked the frightened pupil.

"Because I guessed that the Examiner would ask me to make an omelette, and I hate cooking," Frances answered. The First Mistress looked angry and came close to the child, towering over her she spoke

"You are to stand for your meals for one week, starting with supper." In anger she left the cooking hall. Poor Mother Stanislaus was instantly sympathetic,

"I had no idea that Mother Thérèse would react with a punishment, apologise," encouraged the kindly teacher.

"No, Mother, I won't. I'll stand for meals. She hates me and I hate her," said Frances. Suppertime came, and when the small bell sounded to seat the children, Frances remained standing. A child in punishment could not join in any allowed conversation among other children until an apology was accepted, or until the punishment time ended. For one full week Frances stood for every meal, ignored by her colleagues. The punishment ended on a Sunday.

It was a warm sunny day and the children were allowed into the horses's field at playtime. Entering the field was a special treat where the children played, whenever the grass was dry enough. Sometime during the afternoon Frances picked some grass and with another child licked a few blades to prepare for "blowing" the blade, as was the new craze, started by the latest newcomer to the school.

From the schoolroom window, Mother Thérèse saw Frances's game and beckoned an older girl to call Frances's attention to the nun's window. Looking up she saw that Mother Thérèse had ordered her to attend. Frances reported to the duty nun, and got permission to leave the field, and made her way to the First Mistress's office. Mother Thérèse met her on the office landing and immediately asked,

"Are you hungry?"

"No, Mother," answered Frances.

"Then why were you eating grass?" continued the nun as she grabbed Frances's red curly hair. Frances yelled in pain and Mother Thérèse reached for a cane. The sight of the weapon sent Frances into a tantrum, an uncontrollable tantrum.

"I hate you," screamed the child, "others were blowing grass, but you punish only me. Elsie Hackett was doing the same as me, you wouldn't punish her." The nun lashed out with the cane and it made a swish noise that terrified Frances.

"I'll beat you to within one inch of your life," raged the nun and she caned Frances across her legs again and again, across her body, her arms, legs and shoulders. The Mistress's temper rose and showed in her red face. Frances hoped each blow was the final one, but the blows rained on her body, and Frances screamed and kicked and made a brave effort to grab the cane.

"Get up," yelled the hysterical nun, "and wear this for two weeks." Frances looked up and saw that a large piece of brown cardboard was prepared bearing a cord to place over her head. The notice hung across her chest, and in large black ink was written "I AM A COW". Frances was thankful that the beating was over.

She made her way slowly and painfully, with legs bleeding and hands swollen, down the backstairs and along the corridor by the refectory and playroom and out to the walk leading down to the field. By then the duty nun had changed and Frances was very pleased to see Mother Teresa. The kind and gentle nun met Frances as she approached the field gate. Mother Teresa took her to the playground tap, not far from the field. She washed the wounds and listened to the story of the grass. The large notice was too high for Frances's chin. Then Mother Teresa steered Frances to a seat where they sat together, and talked over the problem.

"I was only playing 'blow', everyone else does it. I wasn't eating it, really," said Frances. Mother Teresa spoke quietly,

"Our Lord was punished and he was innocent," she waited for the child's reaction.

"I hate God, I hate Mother Thérèse. I have prayed to God for Mother Thérèse to die or for her to have an operation or something. Why can't she just go away and never come back," cried Frances.

"Pray for Mother Thérèse," she requested.

"I'd never pray for her, only for her to go away," answered Frances, "my fingers are sore, I have a sore head, she pulled my hair, this string is too short round my neck, this board is too high." Frances was hysterical again. The children had gathered around, and Mother Teresa lengthened the string of the board to make it more convenient. Bunny offered to help with cleaning her shoes until her fingers were healed. Rosanna would cut her bread. Mother Thérèse relieved Mother Teresa at duty change, and on the way off-duty as Mother Teresa walked quietly away from the playground Frances saw that she had a friend in Mother Teresa, she had a brave and noble ally.

That night as the children knelt by their beds for night prayers Frances tried once again to seek heavenly aid.

"Dear God," she prayed, "please take Mother Thérèse to Heaven. She needs a rest, just take her please, Amen." But God was not yet prepared for Mother Thérèse. Every morning Frances hoped that something would have befallen the First Mistress during the night. She compromised at evening prayers,

"Dear God, if you don't need Mother Thérèse could you just make her very sick for six weeks, and let Mother Lelia become First Mistress, but do something with Mother Thérèse.... please, Amen."

Every morning as the children filed into breakfast they felt intimidated by the presence of Mother Thérèse and each gave her a nervous smile and uttered

"Good morning, Mother." Frances continued to ignore the nun. Soon she would be in the Fifth Class with Miss O'Donnell and felt that she was growing up.

Word went about that there was to be a Military Tattoo in Cork City and that the children were to see it. One evening Mother Thérèse read out a list of names of children who were chosen to go. Frances heard her name called! Her sister Kathleen was called too! It was strange to hear her sister's name. They had grown so far apart over the years. Frances was aware, from other examples of sisters, that one day Kathleen would leave without even saying goodbye, as was the custom. They would in all probability never meet again. Only time would tell.

The possibility that Frances might see Cork City was indeed exciting Could it really happen. Best gym slips were being fitted, brown shoes, cream coloured ankle socks and tartan ribbons for their hair. These gym slips were worn only on Christmas Day and on Easter Sunday. Frances couldn't imagine the City. At night it seemed like a sea of lights from the dormitory windows. Bunny was going too, and Rosanna. But not Cracky Sullivan, she had good days and mad days and so the children named her "Cracky". In earlier days Frances had enquired of Cracky if that was her real name,

"No," said Cracky, "I was baptised Marie," then added, "I don't like being called Cracky," and her eyes filled with tears.

"I'll be your friend from now on, and I'll always call you Marie." Frances kept that promise.

Marie could not read or write but she could keep up a good conversation. Mother Finbarr in the early years tried very hard to teach Marie to read, but without success. One other child obviously mentally retarded, always sucking her fingers and rolling her eyes. Then there was Esther who was an epileptic child. She could not go. The date for the trip was set and confirmed. Frances and Bunny planned to sit together in the coach. Rosanna would sit with Breda. Talking in the dormitory increased, in whispers. Sleepless nights from excitement.

The evening before the big day the children were gathered in the playroom to polish their shoes. It was silence time. Frances had shined her shoes and looked across at Bunny who was talking quietly to Anne MacDonnell although it was silence time. Anne was a beautiful child. Her long jet black hair framed her lovely face. Frances remembered the day Anne arrived. She was so beautiful. Shortly after her arrival, Anne went to hospital, and after many weeks returned. The children were shocked to notice that Anne returned with a glass eye! She still looked pretty. No-one questioned why. It was forbidden to ask personal questions. Leaning across Frances asked Anne if she needed help with her shoes. Mother Thérèse noticed and seized the opportunity to exercise punishment. She moved towards Frances and, taking hold of a pair of scissors that hung from a cord on her waist, she cut at Frances's hair.

Large chunks fell to the floor. The children stared in horror. Frances was stunned. She closed her eyes and hoped it was not too bad. From all that fell to the floor she was frantic. In a cool calm voice Mother Thérèse ordered the child to sweep up the hair.

"Then go to the First Classroom tomorrow morning and polish the floor, you will not see the Military Tattoo." The children whispered that Frances was like someone with a scabby head! Once again, the punishment far exceeded the crime. Later in the dormitory washroom Frances beheld a dreadful sight. Such a mess. Her hair would take months to grow. It was her only good gift. Long wavy red hair. If God made children Monday to Friday Frances felt that she must have been made from leftovers late on a Friday evening! Short, plump, freckles and red hair. Her ability to learn was about all she could boast of. Even that gift was ruined by Mother Thérèse who told the children that a devil lived inside Frances and worked her brain.

"Oh yes," the nun told them, "the devil looks after his own."

The future depressed the child, knowing she still had four years at least to finish school, with Mother Thérèse as First Mistress. Although she knelt by her bed that night for routine prayers, she never moved her lips. She refused to talk to a God who was an obvious friend to Mother Thérèse. Next morning her hair stood up in clumps. It was the most awful sight! She boiled with anger and hatred at the First Mistress.

CHAPTER SIX

The coaches left at 11 a.m. with the children. Frances watched from the classroom window as they drove down the Convent avenue. She felt pleased and excited for Bunny and Rosanna, they promised to tell her all the news on their return. The coaches were soon out of sight, and Frances organised her punishment task.

Later that morning Mother Thérèse walked through and gave her a black stare, but Frances was grateful that silence reigned. While polishing and dusting she thought back over her time so far at Sunday's Well. All of the nuns were kind and helpful. Mother Agnes in the dormitory was an angel. Frances remembered listening to the tick, tick, tick of Mother Agnes's watch during her early weeks of admission. The nun was ever ready to help with making beds, always smiling and encouraging, Mother Agnes was a joy to know. then the teachers, Mother Clotilde, Mother Finbarr, Mother Brendan, Mother Bridget, lovely nuns, caring and helpful. There were nuns she looked forward to knowing a little better, Mother Euphrasia, the kitchen nun who worked so hard to feed the children; Mother Colette, the bakehouse nun who made the lovely bread and scones. Maybe one day she might work with Mother Colette. The Mother Stanislaus who taught cookery and had, by then, replaced Mother Clotilde on her retirement. Another Mother Stanislaus who had charge of the gardens who always picked Frances as a helper on Saturdays. So many children rushed to volunteer every Saturday morning, to week the grounds, and to cut the grass. Mother Stanislaus always chose Frances. When the parlour Nun needed extra help to polish the Community staircase, Frances was always pleased to be selected, and she took tremendous pride in exercising loving care on that splendid staircase. When Rosanna and Frances worked together they stood back and admired the beautiful turned rungs and balustrades. Rosanna loved to impersonate Reverend Mother, and walked with elegance down the fine staircase. The sight of Rosanna swanking down the stairs with her thick black knitted knee length socks rolled down to her ankles crowning the tops of her short black boots, sent Frances into a fit of laughter. Rosanna was such fun. She worked well and played well. She was loyal and had all the traits of a sincere friend.

The staircase rose up in the centre of the Convent cloister, and turned left and right to form a gallery that bounded an upper corridor. Along this corridor the Nuns had their private rooms, called "cells". Heavy oak doors, carved by craftsmen in the Nineteenth Century led into each cell. The vows taken by the nuns on the day of their profession, namely Poverty, Chastity and Obedience were written in calligraphy on an oak plaque on each door. Frances and Rosanna adored the architecture of the Convent. When the polishing was finished, and the children waited to be collected by their supervisor they amused themselves with games, e.g. Confession. Rosanna sat on one side of the stairs and Frances stood in the hall on the other side of the rungs. Rosanna was always the Priest. They had their own private Ten Commandments and they enjoyed the game so much that often the duster had to be pushed halfway into the mouth to suppress the laughter, at the sins they imagined. At the far end of the cloister was the most magnificent statues of Calvary. Rosanna and Frances, whilst washing the cloister floor for Mother Perpetual Succour, put on an Oscar performance of dying by the statues.

"Pretend to stab me," said Frances, "and let some water from the bucket pour down my dress, to show that no more blood can flow, then I'm dead, and I'll appear to you on the staircase. You can be Mary Magdalene!" All too soon they would have to return to the school and to Mother Thérèse.

Frances wondered how Rosanna and Bunny were enjoying the show. Would they pass the Shandon Bells, maybe even hear them ring out. She missed her friends, and longed for their return. Frances was too young to appreciate the great sacrifice the good nuns made when they took their final vows, and gave up personal freedom, to care for underprivileged children, and accepted to go through life without appreciation, even a simple thank you. Frances wondered if Mother Thérèse was tired of being a nun and just couldn't get her clothes off. Rosanna had proof, so she said, that once a nun took her final vows and the Bishop dressed her in her habit, it became "stuck on" and that nuns never went to the lavatory and never needed to wash. they were specially blessed to never get dirty. They don't wear knickers, they don't need them, Rosanna had emphasised. "If," said Rosanna, "you looked up the ladder, when the nun was up there, hanging up the Christmas decorations, you'd go blind!" she warned Frances.

The classroom floor was polished to such a shine that as she replaced the little oak desks and chairs and stood back by the entrance door, Frances saw the reflection of the chair legs in the shiny surface. It was getting near to lunch time and she wondered if anyone would call her, or if Mother Thérèse would call again to check her work. Polishing and dusting was the best punishment anyone could receive, thought Frances. The door opened and Mother Thérèse stood watching Frances, who had a polishing cloth under each foot walking up and down the shiny floor, and with a defiant air that helped the incorrigible child to demonstrate a 'couldn't-care-less' attitude with her head bent over her task. In fact the child was wondering what next would the First Mistress give her to do, or was it time for lunch. At last the nun spoke,

"Clean those windows, inside and outside," and off she went. Frances waited until the footsteps could no longer be heard, she tiptoed out of the First Classroom to glance at the clock in Mother Brendan's section of the largest classroom. The time was 1.15 p.m., well after lunchtime, thought Frances, and she guessed that the only drink or meal that she would get, would have to be when the children returned, about 4 p.m. The windows took her attention. Frances was hungry and upset, angry and disappointed and had no-one to talk to, a dangerous situation. She was in a state of mind whereby, she was about to invest in further punishment, and she knew it. The vindictive feeling controlled her otherwise good nature. Mother Thérèse never seemed to want to compromise, she always used force. Never a word of praise. Why? Frances wanted to know the reason why this religious person could hate her. Frances felt she worked well, played fair, was no oil painting as Mary was, but Elsie was not so great either. Elsie had a huge mouth with buck teeth, Frances's teeth were quite normal. She was certain that Mother Thérèse would burn her at the stake if the law permitted her to do so!

The children heard their First Mistress on a "Sunday morning talk" remind them that a good wholesome discipline was the foundation for a successful life outside. Cleanliness and a good religious base was another important aim to prepare for the challenges of life. Frances felt that the only way she would ever satisfy or please the First Mistress was to sit in a box with a number 39 marked on the lid for the next four years, and as she grew taller she would move into a bigger box, silently, until the day came to leave Sunday's Well! Her head was aching, she was tired and hungry. She glanced at the tin of Mansion Polish, the lid was off. She smeared the flannel with a huge amount of pinkish-red polish and moved to the window, inside first she thought. All over the glass she rubbed the polish. To reach the outside of the window without falling sixty feet to her death, Frances sat on the window sill, with her feet dangling on the inside, and brought the weight of the lower pane down onto her lap to hold her in place. It was then possible to reach up and draw down the upper part of the window. In this way she covered the windows with polish and attempted to wipe it off. She used that routine to clean the four windows in the room. The noontime sun shone warmly on the polish, and dried it. Stepping back inside the classroom she could see the full horror of the floor polish on the glass, and felt quite justified for Mother Thérèse's lack of appreciation for her whole effort.

Mother Clotilde arrived suddenly, and went into endless expressions of praise and gratitude for all that Frances had done.

"But the windows, Mother," said a contrite child, "I thought the polish would shine the glass," she lied, "but now I see that it won't." Mother Clotilde observed the windows for a moment or two then burst into laughter.

"Glory be to God," said the naïve but kindly nun, "sure you meant well. I'll tell Mother Thérèse that we both thought it was a good idea." Frances felt very sorry, she realised the damage affected Mother Clotilde more than Mother Thérèse.

"Mother, on Saturday Rosanna Herne and I will get some paraffin and we will fix them, but you will have to ask for us before Mother Stanislaus asks for us for the garden."

"I'll do that," promised Mother Clotilde. "Go and wash your hands and tidy yourself and I'm going to show you a beautiful cloth that Father Mac sent me from Dublin to embroider. You can help me to choose the colours for the flowers," said Mother Clotilde, who liked Frances, as she did all children, but the nun appreciated Frances's zest for learning, ever since her first week in the First Class in 1939.

Father Mac had sent a box of various coloured skeins of silk threads. The mixtures of greens would do the stems, and Frances enjoyed helping "Tilly" to match the appropriate coloured skeins to the flowers on the cloth, of magnificent quality. Frances had two evenings a week in the Art and Crafts class with Mother Clotilde. She enjoyed embroidery and knitting and crochet. The nun's hands were a gift from God. Anything she attempted she succeeded at. She was expert at imparting her knowledge and skills. Such a gentle person, whose very presence influenced peace and goodwill. The spiritual good of the nun emanated and touched the soul of every pupil. The children had no need to test her weakness. She was a professional teacher, with a keen sense of justice, and a real love for God's unfortunate children. Although she had retired from teaching the infants, she used the same room to store her wool and silks for her art class. The sound of coach tyres on the terrace interrupted the nun and child, engrossed in colour coding patterns on the precious cloth. Frances ran to the window

"They're back, Mother, from the Military Tattoo," she called out. Mother Clotilde folded away her lovely linen for another occasion. Together the nun and the child walked out to the coaches. Frances was chatting excitedly about the possibility of what scenes the children saw, as they drove around town. Not a figment of envy in her heart, just sheer joy that her best friends had been lucky. Bunny and Rosanna ran towards her. They rejoiced in being together again. Bunny allowed Rosanna to tell the story.

"Cork is beautiful," said Rosanna, with a pensive expression on her face. "We saw St. Patrick's Cathedral and the beautiful clock on the Shandon

Bells church," she went on. "The church is so small really."

"Shops everywhere," added Bunny.

"And you know," said Rosanna, "I saw many really poor people. The driver told Miss O'Donnell, who was in charge of our coach," continued Rosanna, "that the poor are everywhere, and that thousands are dead in England, and that the Americans are helping in the War." Bunny looked quite sad. "I'm going to be a nun when I grow up to look after the poor," said Bunny.

"I'm not going to be a nun," said Rosanna, I'm going to America. I want to be rich," she added as the trio joined the ranks for collation. In view of the trip the First Mistress allowed the children to talk at the meal. The chatter of so many voices was a deafening noise. Frances listened to every word told about the trip and how wonderful the Tattoo was.

Noreen Dullon, one of the senior girls, thanked Mother Thérèse on behalf of everyone for allowing the children to go out to visit the Military Tattoo. Noreen was a lovely personality, a tall attractive very slim girl, very helpful to the younger children and always helpful to the nuns. Noreen was a special pal of Kathleen, Frances's sister, and often advised Frances hoping to prevent her getting on the wrong side of Mother Thérèse. After Collation and on the way to evening classes, Frances picked up some news from Noreen.

"Don't tell anyone," said Noreen, "but there are some new nuns coming. One is going to the sewing room and two are teachers. Mother Bridget is going to retire. Keep away from Mother Thérèse and from Elsie Hackett, she tells Mother Thérèse everything," said Noreen, "but you must be good, you are always talking, and Mother Thérèse will punish you," added Noreen.

There she parted from Frances to enter the sewing room. Frances continued on to the ironing room of the laundry to Mother Otteran. Another gentle lady, who had strange mood swings, and the children played tricks on her when they felt insecure. She could be angry and did report at times to Mother Thérèse. She had a bad memory and it was so easy to convince Mother Otteran that such and such a task had been done! On her way Frances considered Noreen's advice and news. The lack of contact with the outside world was a disadvantage, and would prove to be so in future years, when the children would need to come to grips with life's challenges, and the complexities of a modern world. Frances had forgotten what money looked like. Bunny seemed "odd" that hour after her trip outside. Was her visit to the City so traumatic that she felt unsure and insecure enough to frighten her from facing life outside a convent environment in time to come?

Frances regretted her lost opportunity. She felt victimised and inevitably suffered disapproval, rejection and punishment. Mother Thérèse projected her own frustrations and aspirations on her. At every punishment session the First Mistress stressed her determination to beat the child into her personal view of a near perfect adult. Frances suffered from low self-esteem. Mother Thérèse was crushing her spirit, however well intentioned the First Mistress was as a disciplinarian. Frances was well aware that if she smiled sweetly and greeted her warmly every time she met Mother Thérèse, half the battle would be over. She could not and would not "pretend friendship". Other children who took part in that double standard were "creeps" in Frances's opinion. The only wrong Frances was ever guilty of, was, "talking at silence time". In her inevitable state of insecurity from day one, and emotional immaturity, Frances was a chatterbox, and would become a chronic chatterbox. Nothing and no-one would ever cure her. She loved to talk. Talking was actually a therapy for her pent up emotions, and for the release of some of the stress that every child carries, when taken away from familiar surroundings, and a mother's love, a granny's love, aunts, uncles. They were the tribe that cemented her spirit to the world. An institution fed her, dressed her, educated her in an impersonal discipline. A day would come when she would be sent out, like it or not, giving rise to further emotional stresses. In Frances's immature opinion, Mother Thérèse was not worth making any effort for.

The children found Frances a good playmate, she enjoyed singing, dancing and schoolwork, in arts and crafts she excelled. Cookery was uninteresting. History stirred her soul. Reading of the battles that took place and always sorry for the dead and injured on both sides! She enjoyed to read of Elizabeth I. She wondered how Elizabeth would have dealt with Mother Thérèse! Parnell, and his help in the fight for Home Rule and as leader in the Land League had proved that a great deal could be achieved and was achieved by non-violent methods. Violence always 'breeds more violence and contempt', thought

Frances and she felt only contempt for her First Mistress. The existence of violence contributed to a faulty relationship, and propensities for disobedience. The mental violence, in reminding Frances of her mother's death, and fuelling the child's feelings of low self-esteem by constantly giving credit to the devil, who the nun insisted lived inside Frances whenever the child achieved any success.

"Don't worry," Bunny and Rosanna encouraged her, whenever there was need. Frances wondered about the years ahead. God, would she ever be 16 or 17 years old. The hopelessness and the pain without a letter from Granny or anyone in Dublin. Better to dismiss the thought.

CHAPTER SEVEN

Saturday evenings were fun times as a dozen children scrubbed the playroom floor. A very large room with bare floorboards and benches. Possibly fifty feet square. Along one complete side from floor to ceiling a pigeon-holed cupboard contained the children's personal "nick-knacks", a holy picture or a Rosary beads, hair ribbon, hair slides, not much beyond those types of objects were stored there. Each pigeon hole had a number. Frances's number 39 was in white paint. The children respected each other's property and would have to seek permission to pass on any item to a friend or to swap anything. Keeping those pigeon holes clean was the responsibility of each child. The floor was a Saturday evening task. Buckets and scrubbing brushes and floor cloths were shared among the volunteers. A routine was agreed among them, and each girl took a particular patch, until the whole room was spick and span for Sunday morning. It was an exhausting chore.

Weary legs mounted the stairs to the dormitory wash room, to freshen up for bedtime. Baths were allowed only once a week on a week day, for various groups until, by Friday, every child had a bath. The bath house was a huge room near the laundry. A large solid wood table held the correct number of bathing gowns and towels, with the child'snumber marked or embroidered, on the corners, and folded readyto identify. On the far side of the room six smooth steps led down to an oblong pool. It could hold sixteen children at one time. The laundry nun was responsible for filling the bath by turning on two chunky brass taps, hot and cold. The water was heated by an enormous solid fuel boiler in the boiler room next door, where the Nun shovelled coal or peat continually through the morning to reach maximum temperature.

Twelve noon was bath time, and lunch was 12.30. When the bath was filled to approximately two feet deep a huge can of Jeyes fluid was added, and then the children trundled on down the steps, and depending on how hot the water was, would file along each side, wearing a bathing gown with wide arm holes. No-one was allowed to be naked. The jeyes fluid irritated skin and eyes. Faces glowed from smarting cheeks!

There was an art in stripping, washing and dressing without ever showing the trunk! Each child washed her hair and her body with a lump of carbolic soap. While the children washed, an assistant, would place a wooden drainer for the children to step out onto. A white sheeting towel, then wrapped around each child, as she made her exit on to the drainer, and again an acquired art to remove a sopping wet bathing robe, from under the towel. Eyes cast down in modesty!, no looking at another's body while drying, and dressing. For any child who had a period on her bath day, a cancellation was made, and a further appointment in the week allocated. Clean underwear was given only on Saturday evening! Hair was inspected every day by senior girls, and they in turn inspected each other's heads. It was common knowledge that if a girl had a bath while she had her period, she went mad! Hence the cancellation!

There was an Infirmary Room in the school for sick children. Dr. Kiely was the School Doctor. In the case of a serious illness he would attend, and he was a charming man. On occasions, a lady Health Inspector visited the school, and the new children had a health check, some time after arrival. Teeth were checked once a year in general, and no fillings were ever done, only extractions! Oral hygiene consisted of a dipping of toothbrushes, every morning, in salt. Fruit in the diet was almost nil until after the War, then in September/October apple windfalls by the bagful were delivered for the children, from the City people.

Twice a year each child received twelve boiled sweets, Christmas and Easter, and they were saved, and looked at, and saved, for as long as two weeks! Feet were never checked. Shoes were passed on from one child to another according to whether the shoe fitted. Children under twelve years wore boots and older girls wore shoes. On Saturday afternoon all shoes were polished. A senior girl stood by, holding a bucket of liquid shoe black, and each child dipped her shoe brush and applied to the scuffed shoes, and buffed them with the dry end of the same brush. Unless Mother Thérèse supervised, shoe polishing hour was a social occasion. Talking was allowed, and the children helped each other to dip or spit and polish and chat. Older girls went with Mother Teresa to the stocking room, to knit stockings. All the children wore black knitted socks, knee length. Mother Teresa would oblige with black wool and four needles for each girl, and the clinking of steel knitting needles would be heard as the girls knitted away, while Mother Teresa led them in the "Rosary to Our Lady".

Frances was good at knitting and had many times joined Mother Teresa's team, unless she was busy elsewhere in the gardens, or doing the Community stairs. Frances much preferred the gardens or polishing floors, because no-one said "The Rosary" there. Apart from Mother Teresa's "Rosary", all children had to gather every evening, for 6 p.m. to say "The Rosary". Frances found the Rosary the most boring of all prayers, and often wondered if Our Lady was as bored listening to them. She could talk in that way to Rosanna, but not to Bunny, who was all too sensitive to tolerate such remarks. Another long prayer, that Frances believed Our Lady had more than enough of, was the Litany. Mother of Peace, Mother of Joy, Mother of Sorrows, Star of the Sea, "imagine Our Lady listening to all that every evening," Frances said to Rosanna, "and all over the world, our Lady cannot possibly hear them all," she continued. "Imagine anyone saying, Rosanna your great, your the Star of Peace, Mother of Sorrow etc., every day! You'd have to say, Oh shut up, wouldn't you!" remarked Frances. "It's so boring."

Rosanna and Frances had grave doubts about certain matters and it was getting very close to their Confirmation. Sunday afternoon at 2.30 p.m. the children attended church for Benediction. Frances loved that service. It was short, with plenty of hymn singing. The hymns were in Latin then, and the children knew every word. The smell of Incense was liked by everyone. Father Aherne or Father Murphy O'Connor swung the instrument back and forth, sending smoke signals all over the altar, that drifted, and wafted down the aisle to where the children sat. The organist accompanied the children's voices as they sang out "O Salutarus Hostia" and Julia O'Leary harmonised beautifully. Then followed a long litany, Blessed be God, Blessed by his Holy name and somewhere in line was Blessed be her Immaculate Conception.

"That meant immaculate birth," said Rosanna, one Sunday after Benediction.

"Well would it be easier to say birth, and be done with it," said Frances, and the two girls were puzzling over the situation and talking, as Mother Thérèse passed them in the hall.

"I don't think it means birth," joined in another girl, and it developed into a discussion. "Ask Mother Thérèse," said the girl, "she knows everything".

Mother Thérèse took an interest in the group conversation. No-one spoke as the nun approached. Frances wondered if Mother Thérèse did know everything, so she ventured to ask, "What does the Immaculate Conception mean?" The First Mistress gave a smug smile, and grabbed Frances by the hair, and led her out of the hall, still holding her hair into the Fifth classroom.

"Go to the oratory," she ordered Frances, "and say The Rosary for insulting Our Lady," said the furious Mother Thérèse.

Frances straightened her hair and corrected the error,

"I did not insult Our Lady, I only wanted to know the meaning of the words 'Immaculate Conception', Rosanna thinks it means birth and I don't believe that, I wanted you to explain." Mother Thérèse was enraged, she slapped Frances's face.

"How dare you defy me," the nun yelled, "it is a mystery of religion which we don't understand, but you better believe. Now go to the oratory until bedtime," the Mistress ordered.

Frances spent at least three hours in that room called the oratory, a sparse clinically clean room, with one statue, lifesize to Frances then, of Our Lady standing on the head of a serpent. The only window overlooked a housing estate behind the boundary wall. Frances watched the men as they tended their gardens and the children running in and out of their houses, and wondered about Aunt Mollie and her father. If they were dead would Mother Thérèse let her know in one of her brainstorms.

Eventually the Mistress arrived, and asked Frances if she said The Rosary.

"No, Mother," said Frances, "I've no beads." Another slap across the child's face, and Frances could take no more, she grabbed the front of the Mistress's habit and shouted,

"I hate you, I hate The Rosary, I hate the Immaculate Conception, and I am not going to be a nun, I'm going to marry the devil." Mother Thérèse became strangely calm.

"Go to bed," she ordered. "I wash my hands of you," she added and walked away.

Frances went crying to the dormitory. Rosanna had kept some bread for her.

"Eat it in bed," said her friend. "The new nun comes tomorrow, she might be nice," said Rosanna.

Next morning the children met the new nun,

Mother Good Counsel. They liked her instantly. Her eyes were as a beam of love, warmth, friendship. She looked so young. Their behaviour, so typical of the children in care to cling, and to maul, as if starved of attention, and desperately insecure, this lovely young, new spirit, could dispel all their fears, and heartaches. Within days Mother Good Counsel's influence took effect. Sports, tennis and rounders, were to be played, and the new nun could run and jump and chase the ball as any fourteen year old could. Tennis and rounders were new games to the children. Mother Good Counsel acquired the tennis rackets and balls. Playtime was Heaven. All through the month of August when the classrooms were closed for the summer break, and when the weather obliged, the children exhausted themselves with the new games. If the selfless dedication to care, by the nuns, was the heart of the school, and the children the vessels that carried their love, then Mother Good Counsel was the oxygen that kept their spirit alive and happy. The whole school admired her.

The children identified with that beautiful young nun. She changed their dull uniforms to brighter colours, and a modern style. The girls in their teens took an interest in their appearance. Mother Thérèse gave in to popular demand for longer hair styles, pretty slides for their hair, nice soap and toothpaste. The black boots were eliminated. Permission to talk at mealtime every day, and not just when Mother Thérèse felt so inclined, became the rule.

Frances felt happy, and found she could tolerate dull times by looking forward to Mother Good Counsel's duty hour. A few new girls arrived, two were from England. Elsie and Biddy. dark haired beauty. She reminded Frances of Snow White. She was so refined, and very charming. Elsie confided in Frances that she was Jewish. The children had no knowledge of the suffering and the murders of Jewish people and their lovely children, through the war years Elsie had known pain, Frances could feel that.

In whispers Elsie told Frances that her broken arm that she arrived with, was very painful, and that she would not want anyone to know that she was Jewish. Elsie was given instruction in the Catholic Faith. She had a sad, wistful look that Frances felt she needed a friend who would not ask questions. Instead they chased around the playground benches and raced up and down the playground. Elsie's arm was in plaster, and within weeks Dr. Kiely removed the plaster. Exercise soon brought complete recovery. Elsie's First Communion Day was made a day for her to remember. She was baptised the day before, the children loved her. She grew very tall and elegant and always remained a gentle girl, but never lost the sadness from her beautiful dark eyes.

Biddy was an absolute extrovert. Her English accent was terribly 'frightfully frightfully'! The bombs in London had something to do with her arrival. Frances found her very stimulating. Biddy loved reading and Frances who was notorious for throwing the bullets other children made, obliged Biddy one day by asking Mother Lelia, the Second Mistress, for a book to read.

There was a grand bookcase in the Inner Hall. But only the older girls were allowed to take out a book on Sundays. Frances and Biddy were twelve years old. Permission was granted for any book, except from the top shelf.

Noreen Dullon was in charge of the library books, and the girls pestered Noreen for a prohibited book! Each Sunday Noreen handed out "Katie's First Term", or "What Katie Did Next". The content was interesting, great adventures, the vocabulary certainly helped their essays in time. Biddy taught Frances some of her poems from her school in England; a favourite was:

" The Two Little Chickens

Two little chickens, one bright Summer's day
Said one to the other, no longer we'll stay
We'll steal out of the barn, and run all around,
And find plenty to eat, as we scratch the ground.

Their mother, she called them, no attention they
     paid
What care we for Mother, she's only a tease
The rest may stay with her, we'll do as we please
But a hawk soon caught sight of them straight
     down he flew
The chickens were frightened, but what could
     they do.
He pounced right upon them, and stole them away
And they have never been seen, since that terrible
     day!"

Biddy was the best, and loyalist friend. She was afraid of no-one. Biddy told them stories of England. Frances enquired about Cheltenham and Oxford, but

Biddy had not seen those places, only heard of them. Saturday tasks were happy times for Frances, Rosanna, Bunny, Biddy and Mary. any combination, or any two from that team, guaranteed fun, and a good job done. They were all in the Fifth Class under a new nun, Mother Philomena. School didn't commence until September, and the year was 1944.

One Saturday Mother Stanislaus chose Frances, Bunny and Mary to tidy up the Nun's Cemetery. A pretty little resting place, a fair distance from the school building, but close to the bakehouse where Mother Colette had charge of making the bread. The little cemetery was bounded by a high stone wall. The walls were covered in the most heavenly perfumed showers of yellow roses. A little bench in a secluded corner made a perfect spot for quiet reading, and the girls always approached cautiously in case a nun was reading there.

Gravelled pathways were weeded, and the grass was cut neatly. With plenty of time to spare before the bell, the girls would enjoy rides in the wheelbarrow, hide and seek behind the large statues and they never missed a request to "Little Nellie" to make them grow taller.

"Little Nellie of Holy God" was a sickly child of three and a half years when she arrived at the Convent in 1906. Her mother had died of tuberculosis. She was a remarkable child, very bright for her age and showed an ardent desire to receive her First Holy Communion. She was very frail and suffered pain. It was unusual at that time for a child to receive Holy Communion under the age of eleven years. The following year a Jesuit Priest visited

Nellie and after several interviews, he, together with the Bishop of Cork, were of the opinion that Nellie was a "special" case. Nellie received her First Holy Communion on 6th November 1907. Up to her death on 2nd February 1908 Nellie received Holy Communion almost every day. She was buried in the City Cemetery, and very soon her burial place became a place of pilgrimage for the people of Cork. Permission was granted a year later for Nellie's body to be exhumed, and reburied in the Convent Cemetery. Her body was found intact. Up to this day Little Nellie's room and her grave are visited by people from all over the world. Children from Ireland and overseas visitors continue a devotion to Little Nellie.

Frances and her pals kept Nellie's grave very clean and swept out the mosaic covered grave. They took turns to lie down in Nellie's grave, saying aloud,

"Please Little Nellie, make me grow another two inches". Frances was the only sceptical one in the group.

"Nellie is not a Saint," Frances said on many occasions, "bet she is withered by now," she'd add. Well, Mary and Bunny grew two inches taller than Frances, and that compounded Bunny's feelings that Nellie should be a "Saint". Little Nellie's grave was very special to the children.

Frances, Bunny and Mary tended all the graves with great care. The nuns were buried there and Mr. James Hegarty had a very lovely tomb. James Hegarty, the Mayor of Cork 1870: He truly loved children.

The girls read and re-read the dates of death, and

wondered how deep the coffins were buried, and if the Nun was withered or had hands left. Frances had a special worry about any nun being buried, who, maybe, was asleep, and looked dead and got buried! Assured by Mary that the nun had to be dead, or she would have woken up, when she was lifted into the coffin. Frances went from grave to grave knocking three times on each, and listening for any response.

Going on her round, one Saturday, Frances moved to a grave behind the James Hegarty grave, with its large statue of the Good Shepherd, and she beheld a shrouded body, lying on the grave. She fell in a faint and hit her head on the stonework base of the statue. She came to, and found Bunny crying, and accusing Mary of murdering Frances. Mary laughed hysterically, and Frances joined in when she realised that the corpse was Mary, who had wrapped herself in a sheet she had taken from her bed, and folded that morning, to carry out her plan!

CHAPTER EIGHT

Summer break was over and the children were informed of their new classes. Frances heard confirmation of her move, to the Fifth Class, along with Rosanna, Breda, Mary and Bunny, many other girls too, her pals mattered to her. Miss O'Donnell, the lay teacher who generally taught the Fifth Class was transferred to the Fourth Class as Mother Bridget had retired. Miss O'Donnell had been teaching the Fifth Class for close on twenty years and she was exceptionally good. She cycled to the Convent every morning, hail, rain or snow, and the children of every class knew her very well. She was a slim good-looking lady.

"Hello Miss" was heard, as children made their way to the classrooms from the hall. If Miss O'Donnell was saddened by her new project of preparing eleven year olds for the Fifth Grade after so many years as teacher of the lower seniors, she did not show any sign of remorse. She knuckled down with her new pupils and the new year began.

The girls who had hoped to be Miss O'Donnell's girls were a little sad. Past pupils had talked of Miss O'Donnell's perfume, that "Miss" gave everyone a spray. She taught her girls about make-up, and demonstrated with her own make-up. The children were not allowed to use such things, but "Miss" considered it useful information for the girls when they eventually left the school. The girls loved to see the lace edging on "Miss's" petticoat when she crossed her long slim legs, and sat upon the table to discuss a point. She never caned anyone. The children obeyed "Miss" and generally looked on "Miss" as a good teacher, and a good friend. Once, when a girl asked "Miss" why she never used the cane, "Miss" took a moment to answer, and said with a smile,

"No, I don't cane any of you, life has been hard enough for you all already." She kept her girls informed of current events in Ireland and she enjoyed history lessons. Frances appreciated that Mother Philomena would probably be as good as "Miss" had been with past pupils, but she was sorry to lose Miss O'Donnell.

Mother Thérèse walked into the Fifth and Sixth classroom with Mother Philomena. Noreen Dullon, a Sixth girl had written Cead mile Failte (one hundred thousand welcomes) on the blackboard. After introducing the nun, Mother Thérèse left the room. The nun smiled and looked around. Twenty children in the Fifth year and six girls in the Examination Class. The School Leaving Exam was taken in June, and the teacher had nine months in which to prepare them. Mother Philomena was a tall young nun. She seemed an easy target for any teaser and they were ready to test her weakness. The nun had a lovely smile and was very affable. The morning was interesting and hard work was certainly appreciated by Mother Philomena. The lunchtime bell rang and everyone ran to line up in such a noisy and chaotic manner, but Mother Philomena clapped her hands together, and in a loud firm voice called everyone to order.

"Girls, girls, please! Is that how you usually

behave when a bell rings. Now return to your seats, and when I raise my hand, walk, do not run, and go one by one, starting from the front row and the second row follow on, in an orderly fashion and do not stampede ever again." The teasers lost the battle, and Mother Philomena won their respect.

Lessons in the Fifth class were enjoyable and the new teacher was an expert at stimulating even the laziest pupil. She was generous with praise, and she had a wonderful sense of humour. Mother Philomena was gifted at imparting her knowledge. Maths was made a game instead of a frightening chore. History became alive and in Geography she encouraged map tracing. Globe handling helped the children's interest so much, that the sound of the bell to end classes brought a chorus of "oh no" from a regretful group.

Mother Philomena had lived in England, and told stories of interest about industries and background incidents. Scotland and Wales and Northern Ireland all added to the wonder of mountain lakes and glens.

Thursday afternoons were devoted to music. Mother Philomena used the blackboard to write up the scale notes. DOH RAY ME FAH SO LA TE DOH in the order of the tune, and in no time the children were ready to put words to music! Mother Philomena was full of energy. She took an interest in the general life of the school and wherever she could bring about or influence change for the better she did her best to achieve results. She was horrified when she noticed that the children were given uncooked black pudding to eat at lunchtime! The kitchen Nun agreed to cook it to a crispy tasty meal. Gruel disappeared.

Porridge, with milk and sugar became routine, and tea instead of warm milk was enjoyed by all. Life was improving at Sunday's Well, in many ways!

The older girls began to take notice of the Altar Boys. Fantasy romances were born! The only time a girl could be near a boy was at the Altar Rail as he held the brass plate under her chin as she received Communion each morning. There were three young boys to approximately thirty five girls ages 13 to 16 years and all were in love with the three boys! Father Aherne noticed a one hundred percent rise in the queue for Holy Communion. It was expected that a girl would keep her head bowed in prayer after returning to her seat, instead, eyes of returned communicants burned through the Altar Boy who was quite oblivious of the whole affair!

One morning these young ladies' dignity fell to an all time low, and any interest the boys may have had in them, in the girls' fantasy world, must have gone forever. The Mass was over, and as the children began to leave the church in order, starting with the four year olds, from the top benches and on down the centre aisle, in age, and out into the cloister beyond the church exit, the piercing screams of the young ones raced back into the church, falling over each other, on and around they ran, and screamed, all the children were in total hysteria. Some fainted, they ran wildly over the main altar. The nuns hurried to protect them, if they could ever collect them! The children were as demented patients! The nuns were horrified. They tried to grab the older girls to find the reason, various answers were given. Frances was caught by Mother Bonaventure,

"What is the matter," said the kind and gentle nun, searching the child's face for a quick and clear answer. Frances was petrified.

"Germans, they are in the cloister!" Mother Bonaventure looked in amazement. Rita ran by, the nun grabbed her.

"Rita, Rita, what is wrong?"

"A monster in the cloister!" Children were huddled together in the Confession Box shaking with fear. It took over an hour to bring the children together. Two nuns went to investigate and returned to explain the position to the sobbing children and to allay their fears.

"There are no Germans," said the Nun, "and no monsters," she added, "The war is over and all the Germans are dead. The only thing unusual that the small ones saw were four kittens! No-one knows who owns them, or where they came from. They were not monsters, only kittens. Now line up for breakfast." The children were n ot convinced that something awful had not been there.

Many of the nuns stayed to comfort and reassure them. School for that day was cancelled and only when the children were released to the playground did any confidence return. Next morning on the journey through the cloister the children were very wary and the First Mistress had to constantly encourage them along into the safety of the church. The rumours spread, from "huge Germans" to "four devils", disguised as kittens, to the Devil who stood in the cloister saying "Don't go to Mass anymore!" The children believed that the nuns had seen the huge Germans, or a monster, or a Devil and were hiding the truth from them, so that they would not be frightened. Mother Brendan reassured the children and spoke to the fifteen and sixteen year olds. They listened with respect to the concerned nun, but the girls had their own ideas of the evil, and no-one could successfully water down whatever idea they had conceived.

Not too long after the church episode, another terror struck the highly imaginative minds of the children. It was a warm and sunny afternoon, lessons were in progress and the Fifth Class heads were bowed over essay writing. Silence prevailed. The teacher was busy marking the history answers from the previous day's work. Suddenly a girl screamed in terror, and it instantly spread among the whole class who jumped over seats, and raced through the intercommunicating doors, into the Fourth Class, and in minutes petrified children from every class were rushing in panic, to the staircase in the First classroom, and falling over smaller children as they headed for the open terrace. Absolute panic spread so rapidly to the lower classes. The teachers were speechless. Children questioned had no idea why they were running and screaming. Many small children were pushed down the stairs in the stampede. The helpless teachers tried to calm the older girls, to bring order, and discover the cause. Outside, the children grouped together to find security in unity. Mother Good Counsel viewed the mayhem from the sewing room door, that opened onto the Second Classroom. Kathleen O'Shea and Noreen Dullon, her right hand and most sensible girls, brushed past her to join the children as they fled the classrooms, and ignored their nun's presence. On down to the playground they ran to join everyone from five classrooms. Then suddenly two men appeared at the top of the walkway to the playground. They wore helmets. The epileptic child had a fit! There was nowhere for the children to run, except up towards the helmeted men. The screaming resounded through the houses of the people who lived near the Convent in Sunday's Well. Then some nuns arrived and joined the men. It became clear to the firemen that the children were afraid of them. The nuns joined the children and explained to them that the men were from the Fire Brigade. That they were fathers with children of their own at home. They were not helmeted Germans.

"The cause of the panic was fire, in the fuse box in the hall, outside the Fifth Classroom," explained a nun. "The girl who screamed had seen the smoke coming under the classroom door." The nun added that in future the children would learn fire drill and that the firemen suggested that a new metal staircase should be installed, very soon, on an outside wall, with an exit door from all floors. Considerable damage was done in the hallway, but the Fire Brigade had done a very good job.

Over several weeks after the fire the whole school was rewired and the children made friends with the electricians. Though the children were calmed by the reassurances of the electricians, the fear and panic would live on in their minds for years.

Some weeks later the Confirmation Class List was made known by Mother Thérèse. Frances, Bunny, Mary Crumlin, Biddy and others, twenty in all. Catechism was learned in detail. Frances learned about clandestine marriages (Registry Offices) and the Six Precepts of the Church and the Seven Deadly Sins - Pride, Covetousness, Lust, Anger, Gluttony, Envy and Sloth.

"How could anyone get through a day without sinning somehow?" Frances said to Rosanna. Bunny absorbed every word the instructing nun put forward. Rosanna would nudge Frances to look at Bunny's face in any lesson. Bunny believed every word put forward by Mother Thérèse who took the task to prepare Confirmation Classes.

The personality clash between Frances and Mother Thérèse was probably the basic reason for Frances's determination to use every lesson to day-dream. Mother Thérèse talked about the Holy Ghost enlightening them as they would be confirmed by the Bishop, as Soldiers of Christ, in the battle against the devil. Frances day-dreamed a battle scene, with Mother Thérèse leading the Holy Ghost Soldiers out in the field and Frances leading the Devil's team against her, carrying banners of the Seven Deadly Sins. Frances's soldiers would be Rosanna, Mary Crumlin, Biddy, Elsie, Mother Teresa, Mother Clotilde, all dressed in kimonos with chrysanthemums in their hair all carrying garden tools and Bunny would be dressed similarly, by force, of course, and trailing behind, crying! Mother Thérèse would have a team led by the Holy Ghost dressed as a huge white bird, that hovered over Elsie Hackett, Breda, Maria Lacey, Noreen Dullon, Kathleen, all the "goody goodies" all dressed in Confirmation dresses and holding banners bearing a picture of a white dove and the words "I'll beat you to within an inch of your life" written in big letters as they closed in on Frances's team.

Bang! The cane hit the table, as Mother Thérèse brought Frances back to earth.

"Frances Donnelly, what are we talking about?" The pupil took a chance,

"The Holy Ghost and em, em," Frances blinked and pulled back expecting the cane to swish across her body.

"Yes," yelled the First Mistress, "the Holy Ghost will alight on each of you, as he did on the apostles. The Bishop will anoint each of you with Holy Chrism and giving you a new name, you will be confirmed into the Army of Christ. The Holy Ghost will fill you with wisdom and knowledge to fight Satan!" Frances had no intention of joining any army that Mother Thérèse had a part in. The lessons were stressful and the teacher was always overbearing. Again the nun addressed Frances.

"What is a Christian, come on, tell the class, let the devil inside you speak to us." Frances smiled, more from embarrassment than arrogance as she looked to Rosanna beside her.

"Em, anyone who follows Christ, I suppose," said Frances, half expecting a wallop from the cane that lay across her desk, but one end held ready in the nun's hand.

"And who do you follow, my lady?" asked the nun as she looked about her with an air of autocracy so typical of her.

"I don't know," teased Frances. A "breath releasing" sound from the classmates only served to stimulate further defiance. Frances felt that Mother Thérèse was using her for ridicule and the child's emotional immaturity was a handicap in the game.

"I don't know who to follow," said Frances, "You follow Christ, but I don't want to be on your side. Elsie Hackett will follow you. I don't know Christ or the Holy Ghost, I can't see them," Frances continued in a quiet but insolent manner. She knew she could never get away with such behaviour. Mother Thérèse stared at her, and the children waited for the cane to be used on their volatile classmate.

"That, children, is the devil talking from inside her. We will ignore him. He is using Frances to be a disturbing influence on the class." Then to Frances she said with a satisfied air, "you will receive three straps each night for three nights," and she proceeded with the religious instruction.

Frances was left with her thoughts. How humiliating to be flogged at the age of twelve and a half years. She knew it had to hurt and pain. She had seen other girls get it. She had recently been removed to the lower dormitory where Mother Thérèse was in charge. No Mother Agnes to defend her there. God was certainly not on her side. As the class dismissed, Bunny assured Frances that she would pray for her.

"Don't bother," said Frances. "I don't need any prayers."

"That's the devil," said Elsie Hackett and Frances flew at her, grabbing Elsie by her long hair. Both girls fell to the floor. Frances held her down on the floor kneeling on her.

"Listen you big mouthed, buck teeth Pet Lamb, there is no devil in me. Thérèse hates me because I am smarter than you. I don't smile and creep around her the way you do. In future keep away from me, and try closing your big mouth." Frances stood up.

"I'll tell Mother Thérèse," sobbed the Pet Lamb.

"Tell tale tat, tell tale tat," called some of the girls after her.

Frances felt better that she had released her emotion. She was not looking forward to "three of the best" that night. She couldn't eat her supper. All beatings were hurtful, painful and humiliating. This flogging was an extra fear. It was a first time flogging for her and fear of the unknown is always more stressful. The children were supportive and expressed their sorrow that she had to go through it. Bunny cried non-stop. Frances was not sure if Bunny's tears were from sympathy, or in fear of the devil that she was bound to believe lived inside her best friend. Rosanna was sad and silent. Biddy said that if Mother Thérèse ever gave her the strap that she would run away first. Frances decided to grin and bear it, and to show Mother Thérèse that she didn't care.

Seven o'clock, and the dormitory door opened.

"Here she is," whispered Rosanna, "good luck," whispered a tearful Mary Crumlin. the nun folded back the bedclothes and turned up the little cotton nightdress. Frances bit her bottom lip and squeezed her pillow. Lash, the bottom of her body jumped involuntarily, lash, and lash. The nun replaced the bedclothes over the child's body, and walked away. Frances lay there in agony. The dormitory door closed behind her.

"Are you alright?" asked Biddy. Frances looked up.

"Yes, thanks, bit sore, but I don't care."

"You're not supposed to talk in the dormitory," called out a goody goody.

The children slept and Frances cried with pain 'til the early hours.

Next day she felt better but the thought of two more nights of pain, from that spiteful nun, filled Frances with hatred. that day she played well and the usual pals were as loyal as ever, and others joined in sympathy. Cassie Hyde told Frances that she admired her.

"I'd die," said Cassie, "if she beat me." Night time seemed to come all too soon and the trauma of the flogging upset many children. They were crying before the nun arrived. Back with the bedclothes, up with the nightie, lash, lash and lash. The nun retreated to the solitude of her own room to say her night prayers, and Frances said hers,

"Dear God, I know you hate me, but could you let my mother help me if she is up there. If you don't let her help me, I will follow the devil, and become a Protestant. I will leave here, and Ireland, and I will go to England and become a Protestant. Amen." While her bottom throbbed with pain Frances fell asleep.

One more night to get through and the flogging would be over. Next day the Confirmation Class heard that canon O'Keefe was to examine their Religious Knowledge for the coming ceremony. Frances had little interest in her Confirmation Day. It was ruined by Mother Thérèse anyway, as Instructress. Frances was angry with God for his obvious deafness to her prayers, as for the Holy Ghost, she could not make sense out of that at all. Frances had an enquiring mind. She wanted facts, no baby stories. However, she enjoyed exams, and derived satisfaction in showing off how much she knew.

"The last night of the floggs," as Rosanna put it. Mother Thérèse was never late. The bottom of Frances's back was very sore already and she was dreading the three lashes. They came harder than ever, as if with the final night's drama the nun had to excel in her effort. Frances screamed, and the nun walked coolly away.

The hatred burned in the child's heart for that unjust autocrat. For weeks Frances limped about holding the bottom of her back and hating Mother Thérèse day by day.

The Canon arrived on a pre-arranged date and the girls were ready and waiting in the Fifth Classroom. Rosanna had seen Mother Thérèse in the hallway smiling sweetly at the Canon. Earlier in the hour Mother Thérèse had reminded the girls that she had done her very best for them, and that she hoped they would not let her down. Frances soaked up that final remark, she wanted to humiliate that nun more than anything on earth. She was prepared to be dropped from the class if she could humiliate her instructress.

The Canon arrived and sat down alongside Mother Thérèse. The nun glanced round at her class and proudly presented Else, a convert. Elsie felt embarrassed. Elsie Hackett, the Pet Lamb, was invited to say the Creed by the Priest. Any child of eight years could have said the Creed thought

Frances, but Pet Lamb was walking on air to impress Mother Thérèse. Many questions were asked and answered, and the Priest was in great form. Mother Thérèse was smiling charmingly and Frances still nursed a painful bottom. The Priest looked around and, pointing to Frances hidden away at the back, disinterested and sullen, asked

"Do you know the words the Priest says as he goes from one Communicant to another, each morning at the Altar rails?"

"Yes," teased the insolent child.

"Well, come on, tell us."

"Corpus Dominastrum Jesu Christi, Custodiat animam Tuam invitamiternam. Amen." She glanced at Mother Thérèse's smiling face, and hatred welled up in her heart for her First Mistress.

"Wait, Father," said Frances, the class stared at her, "In English it means 'Let's eat, drink and be merry, for tomorrow might never come!"

The class roared with laughter and so did the Priest. Mother Thérèse had her hand to her mouth, she was dying of shame. Frances laughed with everyone else.

"Who taught you that one?" asked the Priest of Frances.

"Mother Thérèse told me," lied Frances. She knew she had invested in more trouble but she didn't care any more. The Priest explained the Latin phrase. Frances and the classmates already knew that answer.

"May the body of our Lord Jesus Christ preserve you to life everlasting. Amen." Mother Thérèse was red-faced in temper. The Priest praised their effort

101

and was pleased, he said, to correct the only wrong answer, as it was an important one!

The First Mistress escorted the Canon to the parlour for tea. There were two elegant rooms for receiving guests in the Convent. St. Teresa's Parlour and St. Finbarr's Parlour. It was most likely that the Canon was given high tea in St. Teresa's, where most important guests were taken. Frances was familiar with surroundings in either parlour. The magnificent oak table and chairs; the cake stands; the tapestry stands; beautiful carved writing desks; the elegant chairs of the Victorian era, scattered about on the fine rugs that didn't quite cover the highly polished oak floors. Furniture and accessories matched tastefully. The high-ceilinged bright rooms were not over furnished. Functional pieces, that related well in character and appropriateness to the Convent in general. The atmosphere in the parlours and throughout the Convent was serene. The Canon was allowed to take his meal in peace and the First Mistress returned to the Confirmation Class. Frances expected to be punished. On that occasion she felt she deserved whatever was intended by her First Mistress. Rosanna assessed the situation, and was of the opinion that Frances would be dropped from the Confirmation Group. Mother Thérèse made no reference to the problem. The girls filed out of the classroom and the First Mistress assured them that the Canon was delighted with their depth of knowledge. Frances was amazed at her good luck. Day by day she expected her Mistress to strike out.

CHAPTER NINE

The date for the Confirmation was set for 9th June. White dresses and veils, white socks and white plimsoles were dug out of storage. The dresses had been worn over many years by Confirmation girls since the late Nineteenth Century. Made of the purest Irish cotton the girls were too young and uninformed to appreciate the elegance in design nor the history of the dress. The dresses were stored well in tissue paper and boxed neatly. Fitting the girls with the correct attire and laundering and pressing their pretty classic designed dresses took time and effort and good humour.

Frances felt very excited at the prospect of seeing Cork City from the coach window on the way to the City Church. But the morning dawned overcast, and the rain fell. Torrential rain fell as the girls rushed one by one, from the school main door to the coach door while the kindly driver held an umbrella over her head. Before the coach had driven the length of the avenue, the windows were steamed up. The driver's window was clear enough, but for the majority of the passengers Cork City was out of view.

Frances and her colleagues enjoyed the joke and were convinced that Frances's behaviour had upset the Holy Ghost and rotten weather was her punishment. All but Frances had seen Cork City on their trip to the Military Tattoo.

The Holy Ghost and Frances were not friends on the morning of her confirmation. She agreed to take the name of Mary Finbarr at the Ceremony. Mother

Finbarr gave anyone who took that name a beautiful picture for her prayer book. It wasn't cupboard love, Frances did like Mother Finbarr anyway. Most of the girls received prayer books or beads or pictures from relatives to celebrate their Confirmation Day. Frances received nothing from any relative. She often wondered if in fact they were all dead! Mother Thérèse gave each girl a medal on a pretty chain. 'Souvenir of My Confirmation Day' was engraved on the reverse side. A picture of the Holy Ghost on the front! Frances decided to pack the Holy Ghost into her pigeon hole number 39, as soon as she could on return from church. If I cannot look at Cork City because of your mood, I won't look at you either, thought Frances as she hung her medal back to front while on the coach.

The church was enormous compared to their own school church. An usher guided the children to the top of the church into the two front benches. No doubt a kind and thoughtful gesture by the church administrators. The girls were too naïve to notice the privilege, or to appreciate the kindness shown to them. The Cork people were well aware of St. Finbarr's School at Sunday's Well and though their lives were not easy in the late forties, they rallied to help the nuns whenever they could, financially. The children were not aware that they were underprivileged, or in any way deprived. Certainly they understood that there were family problems, or death of a mother, or both parents that necessitated their "in care" situation. To feel inferior, to the Cork City children around them, in that beautiful church that morning never entered their innocent heads.

Frances's lack of self esteem stemmed only from Mother Thérèse's comments and punishments. Before the Bishop entered the great aisle the whole congregation chatted to each other as if in a huge market square. According to the Cork City Examiner Newspaper the following week, and bearing a huge photo of the children, it said that the children from St. Finbarr's, Sunday's Well behaved with reverence and discipline. Miss O'Donnell cut the page out to show to the nuns and children.

The Bishop entered, and sat below the Altar rails flanked by two Priests. The usher beckoned Rosanna and Bunny to lead, and their colleagues slipped quietly from their benches in line. Frances observed the Bishop. A satin-covered mitre sat on his large head. Cream satin with two gold ribbons just dangling from the crown. The gorgeous matching cream and gold chasuble hung from the Holy man's broad frame. His arms were covered in pure white linen loosely hanging in wide cuff ends. The talent and artistic skill of the seamstress, no doubt the Good Shepherd Nuns was very evident. The kings, at their coronation never looked better, thought Frances! The large and capable hands of the old Bishop were engaged in anointing each child's forehead with chrism while holding on to a crosier. Each child knew the procedure, knelt down before the Holy and learned man, spoke her name clearly and in two minutes Frances was confirmed "Mary Finbarr". She waited to feel the Holy Ghost land on her head. Suddenly she heard the usher's anxious voice whisper in her ear,

"Will you go back to your seat!" Frances stood up and stared at her Bishop in query. She wanted to say the Holy Ghost didn't come, what's the matter with him, but a lady usher was pulling her away to her seat.

"Are you alright?" asked the lady as Frances knelt beside Rosanna.

"I didn't get the Holy Ghost," complained Frances.

"He is in your heart," confirmed the lady usher.

"In my heart? But Mother Thérèse told us he lands on our heads!" argued Frances. The kind lady stared at the child, but not in defeat.

"He lands where he likes, no-one ever feels him," explained the lady.

"Thank you," said Frances politely, but absolutely dissatisfied with the lady's theory.

Bunny was on her knees praying fervently. Frances and Rosanna sat back and watched the City children one by one being confirmed. They observed the beautiful silk dresses, white leather shoes with buckles, some wore gorgeous coats in blue or pink, unbuttoned to display the front of their dresses. Their veils and head-dresses were exquisite in design. Many girls were tall and elegant. How lucky they were, thought Frances. She had no knowledge or memories of poverty or affluence or understood that those two imposters controlled the attire. She felt no envy, only admiration. She accepted long ago that she was short and plump, with red hair. She wanted to be tall with long slim fingers. She glanced at Bunny who was deep in prayer. Whatever could she be praying about and for so long, thought Frances. Bunny accepted every teaching at face value. Frances needed to really understand the point. Rosanna had the same demand. Frances was bored with The Rosary and The Litany. She felt it was also boring to Our lady to hear the same prayers day in and day out. It was "creeping" and "pet lambing" to keep on telling God and Our Lady how great they were. She felt that prayers should be "chats" with God. Nor long boring psalms written hundreds of years ago by people who said "art" and "thou" and "allauia". Why not say, "Hello God, did you have a good day, mine was terrible. By the way, I hate being short, but if you have a big plan for me to help others by being short, I could accept it OK." Often the nun would remark "it's God's Will". Frances hated that expression. On the one hand God gave us all a "memory",a "will" and an "understanding" according to the "Retreat Priest", there were many times when Frances wondered if she had any free will!

The good-looking tall girls were lucky. She would even have been happy being good-looking, though short, But God had some weird ideas at times. He never seemed to do things fairly. Heaven had to have plenty of eyes and noses, legs and arms, hair and teeth. Maybe the angels helped him thought Frances, some of those angels were certainly not too good at putting parts together! Now the Holy Ghost had come down to do his part! Or would he? The apostles spoke in "divers tongues" after the Holy Ghost came down to them. Frances wondered what he would do for her. Ten to one he missed her out completely as she was dwarfed by the tall girls! At twelve and a half she stood only five foot one inch. Nothing worked. She asked God, Our Lady, Little Nellie - all deaf by all accounts to her prayers for height! At times she wondered if any of them really existed.

107

The ceremony dragged on and on. The Bishop's mitre was wet along the edge on his forehead. Frances was aching to talk. She nudged Rosanna,

"Ask Bunny did she feel the Holy Ghost," said Frances. Bunny nodded her prayerful head in affirmation! Rosanna and Frances looked at each other in surprise, wonder and gravely worried!

"I doubted that he'd ever come to me," said Frances, "but you are quite good. Do you think it's because you are my friend?" she asked Rosanna as her self esteem dropped even lower. Rosanna accepted that the Holy Ghost came and blessed them with wisdom and left for the next child, in every case. Frances looked forward to discovering her new gift of wisdom. She wondered if the new gift would enlighten Elsie Hackett about the lowness of snitching!

Suddenly, the organ played, and everyone stood up. The lofty ceiling over the aisle and the stone pillars and walls in the splendid church pertained to the marvellous acoustic as the sound of music vibrated in heavenly tone. The whole congregation joined in singing:

"Veni Creator Spiritu
Mentes tu orum visita
Imple Superna Gratia
Quae tu create in Pectora
Que diceris paraclitus
Altissimi Dominum Dei
FONS VIVUS ignius caritas
Et spiritalis in uncito.
                              Amen"

The rain still fell in torrents on the journey back to Sunday's Well. The children were very disappointed. The coach windows were completely steamed up and there was little hope that Frances would see anything of Cork City. No photographs were taken on the lawns due to the weather. Clothes were changed and put away, and nothing special was made of their Confirmation Day.

At a convenient time during each year the children went on a "Retreat". It was a time of enforced silence for three whole days! A sermon was preached every evening by a Redemptorist Priest. The children were encouraged by the Priest's words to look back on their lives and to improve their ways. To strengthen their character to become better Catholics.

The silence was tantalising for Frances. The children enjoyed stories told by the Missionary. Tales of the man who went to Confession on his deathbed! Then the funny story about a man who was given the "stations" for his penance and he arrived home after midnight. When his wife asked him where he had been he blamed the Priest for giving him the "stations" to do as he couldn't find Waterloo Station! No doubt he lived in London!

Many of the Priests had been preaching at Retreats in England and Frances enjoyed stories of England, always hoping for a mention of Cheltenham or Oxford. She never forgot those place names that her father mentioned in glowing terms all those years ago.

Somehow the Missionary managed to fit in a terrifying sermon, usually the last night, as if to leave a lasting affect! Hell and its demons, waiting by the front gate to tempt every girl as she left her school days behind! The demons that moved about in the shadow of the dance halls, and possessed the bodies of young girls! Frances wondered if he was talking about her! Had Mother Thérèse told him to say that? When the Priest finished with a prayer for all souls possessed by a devil she was afraid to look at anyone, she read their thoughts! The idea that lost souls burned in hell for all eternity made no sense. Trillions of people already dead, how many were burning in hell, and where would "Old Nick" put the next lot and so on, how big was that Hell? Another mystery!

School resumed and hard work lay ahead in the hope that when Frances was old enough she would be allowed to take her School Leaving Certificate. School days were very enjoyable. Mother Philomena was an excellent teacher. History was so interesting. The teacher allowed her to read various relevant books to develop unbiased views of battles that took place between Ireland and England. The French promised so much help, but were always too late! Cromwell was an autocrat, a very dangerous man. Elizabeth I was such a strong minded person. Frances admired her as a great Queen of England, if a thieving wench in Ireland. The poor Earl of Essex, Elizabeth was wickedly unfair to him. The O'Neills and the O'Donnells the Earls of Ulster - those nobel knights who loved Ireland. Tired of bloodshed and fighting they fled to the Continent to peace. Thomas Moore, an Irish Nationalist used his pen as his sword. Achieved much for Ireland without violence. In the beautiful poem 'The Vale of Avoca' he wrote about the two rivers that meet in Avoca, Co. Wicklow and his words were so apt in the late forties as they were one hundred years before:

"Where the storms that we feel
In this cold world should cease
And our hearts like thy waters
Be mingled in peace."

Sundays, once Mass and breakfast were over, were spent reading. Frances was seated next to Noreen Dullon. Frances was reading a history book that belonged to Mother Philomena. Noreen was often called to perform some responsible task for the First Mistress, often to post a letter. Noreen placed her book beside Frances for her return. The book was from the library shelf forbidden to anyone under sixteen years. The temptation was too much and Frances picked up the book and started to read. "The Four Feathers." She read for two hours while Noreen was away. It was a beautiful story. On Noreen's return Frances begged to be allowed to finish the story. Her good friend promised to "take out" that book for two further Sundays to enable Frances to finish the story. The story was about a brave British soldier who was assumed a coward by his father and three friends, so he set out to prove his worth. Using her name Noreen "took out" some fine books for Frances to read. The books were enlightening and stimulating for composition at school. Her vocabulary improved and Mother Philomena was pleased with her behaviour and progress. Keeping out of Mother Thérèse's way was not too difficult and altogether Frances was quite content.

Each year Mother Thérèse produced a list of girls who were given a certain coloured ribbon to wear around the neck with a medal attached; red, green, narrow blue and wide blue, between the ages of 13 and 16 years. The colour denoted a girl's achievement in the field of helpfulness, and whether well behaved, and capable of taking charge in the nuns' absence. No nun ever complained about Frances, she volunteered for work every Saturday. Her school work was to the best of her ability, but Mother Thérèse would not give her a ribbon. Mary, Bunny and Rosanna had red or green ribbons. No praise or reward or incentive ever came from Mother Thérèse to Frances. When any hard work was available, she would always send Frances. All work, but no praise!

Frances spent two years in the Fifth class, as she had to be fourteen years old to move to the Sixth and to take the School's Leaving Certificate. English, Irish, History, Geography and Arithmetic were the only subjects allowed. Mother Philomena worked relentlessly to help her Exam girls. Mary and Bunny were not chosen to sit the Exam but Mother Philomena chose Frances, Breda, Rosanna, Pauline, Mary McDonough and Joan Mellerick. As the exam date grew near Mother Philomena worked with the class every extra hour she could spare.

The morning dawned one day in June. Outside in Cork City many children were sitting the same exam. Mother Thérèse supervised in the examination room. All desks were rearranged with wide spaces between them. At 9 a.m. Reverend Mother from the Convent entered the classroom and witnessed the seal being broken on the large brown package that contained the exam papers. She wished the girls good luck and left. Mother Thérèse distributed each paper. Each paper took one hour. With a break for lunch, the exam finished at approximately 3.30 p.m. All morning the clock ticked away the minutes, then the First Mistress called "time up" and collected all papers and distributed the next subject. That evening the girls collected together to discuss the papers with Mother Philomena, and Frances felt confident that she had done well. Results were given in September as a rule.

CHAPTER TEN

The girls remained with Mother Philomena until the end of July and then came the summer break that lasted for four weeks, and were spent playing tennis and rounders and clock golf. Sundays were reading days and Frances wondered how long could Noreen be in a position to help her with the library books. Although she was old enough to read the top row books, her every application was refused by Mother Thérèse. Kathleen had left the school and gone out, somewhere, but not a word of goodbye to her sister. Bunny's sister Joan was gone, with no goodbye. Mary's sister Lily was gone, sisters just didn't matter to each other.

Now Noreen Dullon was leaving and, strangely, Mother Thérèse allowed her to say goodbye one morning shortly after the school exam and before the summer break ended. Noreen was sent to an aunt in Dublin, or so the girls were told. Everyone loved Noreen, she was emotionally very mature, very intelligent, tall and attractive. Her absence left a void in the children's lives. There was no other girl to match Noreen's standing. She was sadly missed. Noreen had always been the Fairy Queen or whatever the major part called for, in any play. She was the natural Dick Whittington. She had a glorious voice, and could harmonise beautifully. It was a sad day for all the nuns and children when Noreen had to leave. She could walk with kings or beggars, and treat each with charm and respect. Her mother died when Noreen was very young and her father went to work in a mill, in Bolton, Lancashire. He lost an arm in an accident in the mill. He could not bear to visit Noreen for she was the image of her mother. He set aside his accident compensation and his savings for Noreen's future. Noreen went on to enjoy a very happy life in New Mexico. She married very happily and had a beautiful family, and wrote many letters to the nuns. Mother Philomena kept her friends informed.

August was ending and Frances wondered what Mother Thérèse had in mind for her final year. She hoped it wouldn't be the kitchen, she hated cookery. The laundry was another painful idea. Then one evening the names were called for work experience. Frances Donnelly, Mary and Bunny - the bakehouse and tomato plants! Fantastic! Frances couldn't believe that Mother Thérèse would or could do anything right for her. She was afraid to look pleased in case the First Mistress changed her mind. What a team! They rejoiced in the lavatory, out of Elsie Hackett's hearing! Mother Colette had a great name for being hardworking but fair in every way. The three girls happily set off one Monday morning to Mother Colette at 8.30 a.m.

The bakehouse was divided into two rooms, an outer room with long shelves on three tiers to store the freshly baked loaves, a section set apart to store at least thirty large sacks of white flour. The Cork flour mills delivered the flour at regular intervals. Mother Colette kept a well stocked cupboard in that outer room. She stored raisins, candy peel, currants, etc. A long hardwood table stood in the centre and on that stood weighing scales to aid cake making. That table was scrubbed daily. Mother Colette loved every item, from floor to ceiling, every receptacle to be spotlessly clean. Cleanliness was a strict rule.

The inner room housed the mixing machine for the dough and for cake mixes. Another enormous well-scrubbed hardwood table with drawers custom built to house large black metal deep baking pans. Each pan could house ten loaves. The table was used for making up the loaves each day. A huge bin to house the freshly made dough. A sink with hot and cold water.

The girls were also responsible for the huge greenhouse with tomato plants. Mother Colette welcomed her three new girls and allocated them to their duties. They could, she told them, swap duties if they wished, as long as the work was done well. Mother Colette was willing and able to do any task with them.

The work was a training to develop a sense of responsibility; to work in association; to respect each other and to obey and respect the person in charge. The nun led her young team and exercised a fair system. The girls were in awe of their teacher. Their loyalty to her and their respect for her grew daily.

Each morning Frances put one and a half sacks of flour into a machine, and one and a half pounds of yeast blended in warm water, a half scoop of salt and cold water. She sealed the lid with the aid of an iron bar and pressed the red button to start the machine in motion. There were many tasks to be done as an everyday routine, until the dough was ready to be moved from the machine to the store bin. She covered the dough with empty flour sacks and left the mixture for a few hours to rise.

The large solid wooden table in the oven room was prepared for making up the loaves. The clean and freshly greased pans were lined up on either side of the table ready to receive the loaves. During "make up loaves" time, many hands made light work. Mother Colette, Mary, Bunny and Frances spent a pleasant hour filling the black pans, and with Bunny's acquired skill at manoeuvring the pans, with the help of a large pliable hardwood pole, twenty-two pans holding ten loaves in each pan, were lined up in tidy rows in a roasting hot oven that measured approximately 18ft by 18 ft. Lifting and shifting each metal black pan, full of unbaked loaves, and hoisting each pan up onto the oven ledge twenty-two times, with the reverse routine one hour later, when the bread was baked, every day for six baking days, was no easy task for Mother Colette who was feather weight, or for any child of sixteen years. No-one complained. The children were happy and usually sang as they worked. Mother Colette worked as hard as anyone and the girls adored her.

The smell of newly baked bread filled the air around the school every day at about 3.30 p.m. Mary prepared her shelves to receive the freshly baked loaves. A step ladder was placed near the three rows of shelves to assist the girls to reach the top shelf. Bunny's face was glowing red by the time she reached the final pan. There was an art in shaking ten loaves forward onto the open arms of a colleague. Although the girls protected their hands with oven cloths, many nasty burns were sustained especially on forearms.

117

The pans were extremely hot when withdrawn from the oven. By 4 p.m. every day the girls were proud of a good day's work as they returned to the school building and left a splendidly clean bakery.

Frances saw very little of Mother Thérèse. Evening recreation was enjoyed either in the playground, the field or in the playroom depending on the weather. In early October Frances heard from Mother Philomena that she passed her School Leaving Certificate and that Mother Thérèse would give that certificate to her on leaving the Convent in due course. One child had failed. She was such a nice girl that she would find her way with success without certification. Frances was very proud of her success and Mother Colette made a delicious sponge cake to celebrate, just for her team. Mary and Bunny and Frances enjoyed to sing while they worked. They sang in chorus each others choice of song. Frances had a favourite: "The Croppie Boy":

"Good men and true
In this house who dwell
To a stranger Buchal I pray you tell
Is the priest at home, or may be seen
For I would speak a word
with Father Green.

The youth then entered an empty hall
Not an only sound,
As if life would fall.
In the gloomy chamber,
Still and bare
Sat a vested priest on a lowly chair.

The youth then knelt to tell his sins
In omni Dei the youth begins
At Mea Culpa he beats his breast
And in broken murmur
He tells the rest.

I cursed three times
Since last Easter Day
At Mass time once I knelt to pray
I passed a churchyard
One day in haste
And forgot to pray
For my Mother's rest.

I bear no hatred
Against living things
I love my country above all kings
So Father bless me and let me go
To die if God has ordained it so."

The verses followed on to show that the Priest was
an enemy soldier and he murdered the Young
Croppie Boy. The Croppie Boys were a regiment in
Ireland's troubled times. It was the historic
background of the song that Frances loved so much.

The tomato plants were an extra task for the
bakery girls. Mother Colette kept the boiler well
fuelled and aired and clean of ashes. Glorious
summer days in the greenhouse, pinching out the
side shoots and picking off the ripe fruit was a
favourite task that appealed to Mary. The girls had
no appreciation of the value the tomato plants were
to the Convent purse. The ripe fruit brought in a

small extra income to enable the nuns to continue their work for the children. Mother Colette taught the girls to make madeira cakes, rich fruit cakes and sponge cake and little fairy cakes. The cupboard was an Aladdin's cave of goodies. Raisins and candy peel, currants and sultanas. They had no appreciation of the monetary cost of such goods. Reducing the stock by handfuls simply meant that Mother Colette would replace them with no problem from some vast store in the Convent! They became expert at opening the cupboard door with a small knife. Then afterwards they simply closed the two sides of the door simultaneously to give the appearance of a locked cupboard. Mother Colette turned a blind eye! The day the girls discovered that their nun was well aware of their little game came in such a manner it left them shocked and ashamed. Mother Colette was going across to the Convent for an hour or so and as she locked the cupboard she remarked,

"Now girls, the fruit in this cupboard is all I have until next week and I need it badly for a special cake on Friday. Please, don't take any and leave that knife alone." And she looked at each girl and at the knife lying nearby! She left them standing, in shock! There was no challenge, no excitement, and the appetite for the fruit diminished. So they turned to the tomato house.

Mary was the slimmest of the group. She found a way to remove a pane of glass, just large enough for her to crawl through and then slipped it into a slot, having removed all seals around the pane on the inside. This enabled one of them on the outside to re-position the pane as soon as Mary was safely hidden among the plants. She picked six luscious tomatoes and handed them out while she slipped eel-like through the small opening and covered her track. A feast of hot bread and tomatoes was a glorious perk of the job. The excitement and the intrigue was the fun. The girls had no real need for food, they were never hungry. They were happy and enjoyed their work.

One morning the three girls were shocked to see a new nun waiting for them in place of Mother Colette by the bakery door.

"Mother Coregia! Where is Mother Colette?" they enquired. "I have taken over from her," said Mother Coregia, "and I know nothing about the work," the nun had tears in her eyes. The girls were shocked, devastated.

"You will have to teach me everything about bread making," said their new nun. The girls stood in shock and at first wondered if it was a joke. But, no, it was no joke. Mother Colette had been moved and Mother Coregia was their new supervisor. Mary was the first to speak,

"Mother, just go and tell Reverend Mother that you hate the bakery, and that Mother Colette must come back." The lovely nun looked at her young team and explained,

"We have to obey and we have to accept change and learn." The girls were torn with sadness at the loss of Mother Colette so suddenly, no explanation given, no goodbye, it was so cruel. Now Mother Coregia was in charge, against her will. They continued the morning routine. Poor Mother Coregia was useless! and the girls felt they had to help her, and to teach her. Mary spoke to Frances and Bunny,

"We'll teach her to make the dough," and then Frances added, "we'll tell her she has to give us currants every day!" The new nun was quick to learn, and although the girls never forgot Mother Colette, and no other nun would ever be as good in their eyes, the girls helped in every way to carry on the good work in the bakery and in the tomato house. Mother Coregia was very "motherly". One day she left the box of raisins on the table and she went to the Convent. The girls had a wonderful afternoon. Suddenly, the door opened, and Frances had her hand in the raisin box. The nun stared in surprise,

"Oh," said Frances, "my hand fell in!" Mother Coregia burst into laughter and wagging her finger told Frances, "I was going to give you all a special treat today, of sponge cake, and a cup of tea, and now I won't. You have spoiled it for yourself, and for the others."

"Oh, please Mother, Mary and Bunny won't mind if I tell you that they took some too, so there is nothing to spoil for them!" Mother Coregia's eyes opened at the news, and at the logic! An hour later she relented and made the tea for all.

Their new nun was always happy to see the shelves laden with fresh bread, and the bakery tables, and floors, and baking pans, machines and dough bin, spotlessly clean. She would make a pot of tea and little queen cakes, for her girls, and they would chat, and gossip on many points. Mother Coregia was older than Mother Colette. The children didn't mind that. Frances related some of her past experiences with Mother Thérèse, and found in Mother Coregia a sincere ally. Mother Coregia took a keen interest in the various tasks. The girls reminded her to check with the kitchen nun for bread requirements for the children's kitchen and with the Convent kitchen nun, for cake and bread requirements for the nuns. They missed Mother Colette, as she always double-checked every roof window in the greenhouse, oven temperatures, and many small tasks that were important, but easily overlooked by the children. The girls shared jobs, and made every effort to prevent disasters, as they knew the risk of bringing Mother Thérèse to the bakery. Frances noticed that the flour was running low. The man from the flour mills usually arrived on time, but for some reason had missed a call. Mother Coregia was pleased to have been informed. She enquired, and to her horror discovered that a strike in the flour mills meant no more deliveries until the strike was settled. Day by day the flour situation worsened, until the girls reached the final bag on the wooden pallet. Mother Colette would have foreseen the problem, and made less bread, and perhaps rationed the bread to prevent a "no bread" situation. Mother Coregia was too new. She became very worried, and upset at the seriousness of the situation. Wringing her hands, she looked to the girls for help.

She left the bakery for an hour, as she did every morning. She suggested that the girls should go to Little Nellie's grave to pray for the flour. Three sixteen year olds knelt by the graveside of the past pupil, and talked aloud to Nellie. Frances explained to Nellie that the flour mill was on strike, and Mother Coregia was very worried,

"Is there anything you can do to help us?"

"We are down to nothing," added Bunny, "we need a batch of dough today, and a double batch on Friday," she went on.

Frances reminded Nellie that she had not grown an inch since the last time she lay in Nellie's grave.

Back at the bakehouse as they entered the outer room Frances had a brainstorm.

"Look," she said to Mary and Bunny, "under the pallet, all the flour." Flour had fallen between the stacked bags over the months, especially as the girls scooped out the extra half bag every morning for the dough, it was impossible not to drop a certain amount, at the speed they worked. Their spirits rose. Bunny went on her knees to thank Little Nellie for finding the flour. Mustering their total energy, they lifted the pallets that normally took the weight of 30 huge sacks of flour. The sacks were made of canvas and tied with string. Once the pallets were moved aside, Mary swept the stale flour into a heap.

"It's filthy," said Frances, "look at this, dust, fluff, strings, cockroaches, mice dirt." Mary was not daunted.

"Pick out what we can see, and the machine will do the rest."

"Little Nellie will do a miracle when it's turning in the machine," said Bunny. Scooping up the stale flour with all its foreign bodies, the girls loaded the machine. They added the salt, the water and the yeast, and lifted into place the heavy iron cover and snapped it into the safety catch. The switch was pressed, and away went the mixture. The girls were delighted with their luck, and Nellie's help! Mary scrubbed the pallets while Bunny and Frances cleaned the floor, and replaced the pallets. In due time the dough was ready to be removed from the mixing machine. It looked OK, while soggy. The girls removed the odd hair grip that showed on the surface! They covered the miracle dough with empty flour sacks, to keep it warm. Mother Coregia returned in the early afternoon. Mary rushed to tell the news.

"Mother, we found that we still had flour, we can make today's bread," Mary's eyes were wide and excited. The incredulous expression on the nun's face turned to a broad smile as she beheld the bin, full of dough. It had risen too!

"You are great, wonderful girls, and I'm going to make you a cup of tea, and give you each a slice of cherry cake." The atmosphere was sheer happiness. Bunny kept thanking Little Nellie. Frances hadn't much faith in Nellie, she hadn't seen much of a miracle over 5 ft 1 inch, in spite of all the requests, and in view of all the times Frances had swept and cleaned the mosaic surface on Nellie's grave, and steered lost visitors on many occasions to where the little one lay she still stood at 5 ft 1 inch.

Tea over, and the girls prepared the baking table to mix the dough loaves. While moving the dough onto the table, the dirt, and the debris became visible. Pieces of hairy string from the old sacks, wet fluff, and worst of all, tiny maggots! Frances called the nun's attention.

"There are maggots in this dough, and string and dirt." Mother Coregia looked at the mixture.

"Glory be to God, what are we to do, we'll poison everyone, get it back into the trolley. We'll dig a hole in the garden, and bury it," said a shocked nun. Bunny was in tears at Little Nellie's game. Mary laughed until her sides hurt and Frances joined Mary in laughter, until Mother Coregia saw the funny side too. Bunny got two shovels from the tool shed. The nun led the way to the back of the bakery, and the girls pulled the trolley of rotten dough to its burial place. Suddenly, as they were halfway there, Frances saw Mother Euphrasia and her girls from the kitchen returning with milk from "The Hill".

"Here come the kitchen girls," said Frances in panic.

"Take it back, take it back," whispered Mother Coregia, "we'll be the talk of the Convent!" The heavy load was dragged back to the starting post, until the coast was clear. Then with aching arms and shoulders, the procession continued on to its resting place.

"Dig here," said a disappointed nun.

"Dig a long trench." The dough was shared out along the channel grave and covered with earth and flattened down. Filled with relief, they returned to the bakehouse. Bunny was upset at Frances's lack of faith in Little Nellie.

"I don't believe in miracles," said Frances who continued to hold a grudge against God for the death of her mother. Mary and Bunny were sure that the devil had spoiled the dough to upset their belief in Little Nellie.

That night the whole school prayed for flour and for the strike to end. Frances was not looking forward to too many sacks arriving, shunting them about was a back-aching task.

Early next morning as the bakery girls made their way towards the bakehouse, they saw the huge flour mill's open truck, with a few bags of flour being unloaded. They ran to Mother Coregia who seemed upset.

"What's wrong, Mother?" asked Bunny.

"Look out the back," the nun whispered. They rushed around to check, and there, the dough had risen again, clear through the soil! They roared with laughter, and with help from the "flour man", they beat it down once more.

"Is the strike over?" Mother Coregia asked the flour man.

"No, no, but children are a special case, and this will help you to keep going." Bunny smiled,

"Little Nellie helped us," she said!

Back to normal routine and busy with bread-making, Mary, Bunny and Frances were a happy trio. Occasionally they would meet Mother Colette, and tell her how much they missed her. She encouraged them to be good, and helpful, and asked them not to let her down.

CHAPTER ELEVEN

One fine sunny warm afternoon in late summer the floors were being washed in the three bakery rooms. Mary had a good voice and was singing loudly:

"Roll along Good Shepherd laundry
Roll along
To the turn of the wheel
We sing this song
When our Nuns go in to pray
St Finbarr's girls will always play
Roll along Good Shepherd laundry
Roll along"

(To the tune of Roll Along Covered Wagon)

Mary stood back to admire her effort. As she turned to move her bucket of water, she screamed in terror, and rushed out through the front door running and screaming. A small white dog had entered her room. She had never seen a dog since a tot. Eileen had no memory of ever seeing a dog. Frances had a vague memory. On and on, and around the cemetery Mary ran, jumping over tombstones, down the back of the bakery along by the boundary wall. With her feet thumping out the terror in her body, she screamed,

"Help, Help," and the little white dog in hot pursuit. Mary dashed through the open back door of the room she had been scrubbing and climbed up onto the flour sacks. The little dog raced in after her, and seeing the bucket of soapy water stopped at once to drink. Mary was hysterical, upon the bags of flour yelling,

"Save me, save me" she and the dog had run two laps around the garden, cemetery and boundary along the back of the bakery. The dog was adorable and just enjoyed a chase and a drink and made his way off. Mother Coregia laughed until tears were pouring from her eyes.

"Come down, Mary," requested the nun.

"No, no, no, shut that door," shouted Mary. Eventually she came down. Bunny and Frances had great fun for weeks following that event. During any silent moment whenever Mary was deep in concentration Frances would shout "it's a dog" and Mary would take off in panic, screaming!

On any wet Sunday afternoon all children were confined to a large playroom. A wonderful surprise was sprung on the children on one of those wet Sundays. A nun arrived who was not normally attached to the school. There were a number of nuns that the children knew by sight, but were "Convent only" nuns. This nun carried a huge box and invited all the children to sit around in rows. The older girls arranged benches in the required order. Mother Lelia joined in, and covered all the windows with dark curtains, and soon the excitement mounted as the Convent nun explained, that the projector was about to show them a film, with sound and music! While the nuns prepared the set up, the children sat in absolute silence and in amazement. All was ready, lights were put out by Mother Lelia, and suddenly the children gasped in shock and delight. The people in the film were moving about and talking! It was magic, fantastic. Frances, Bunny, Mary and Rosanna were enthralled. The film was called "Joan of Arc". The story was so moving, so full of history, bravery and evilness! The surprise was wonderful. The film was unforgettable. It ended in time for Collation, and the discussion on the wonderful story of Joan of Arc stimulated much argument. For the very young children there was very little stimulation. They brought out their little boxes from their pigeon holes and discussed little trinkets of interest.

One particular Sunday Frances, Rosanna, Mary and Bunny were discussing a book from the library, when they noticed a shadow at the playroom window. It looked like a man, he wore a trilby. It was Mother Brendan's duty hour. She was supervising at least one hundred children. Instead of immediately informing the nun, Frances and Mary went outside, thinking on their way out that it was a Priest on his way down from Little Nellie's grave. It was not a usual occurrence but it had happened in the past. The children noticed that the man was not a Priest. He wore a heavy dark unbuttoned overcoat and a hat. He opened his coat for a second or two. Frances and Mary had little experience at communicating with anyone other than the nuns. He repeated the behaviour all the while smiling. The confused girls retreated and shut the door. He hadn't spoken a word.

"Is he German," asked Mary.

"Let's tell Mother Brendan," said Frances. Their nun's face showed anxiety as the girls related the event. Mother brendan called all the children to attention.

"I need silence," she said. "I have to leave you for a while. The older girls will look after you until I return." She sent Frances to find another nun. She ordered the children to stay in the playroom until a nun arrived. She didn't deliberately relay any panic, but the children sensed that there was something amiss. Frances headed for the Kitchen Nun but with no luck. She then popped up the "stony steps" and met Mother Lelia. She greeted the Second Mistress with a request for help for Mother Brendan. Frances related the story to the Second Mistress as they hurried back to the playroom. On along the corridor towards the playroom Mother Lelia asked questions about the silent man who just flapped open his overcoat. They reached the playroom. Mother Brendan was gone some time along the terrace towards the avenue. The children had seen her shadow move along by the terrace windows. It was some time before she returned and assured the children that the police had taken the poor man away. She called Frances and Mary to join her and Mother Lelia.

"Now what did the man say," asked Mother Brendan.

"Nothing Mother, nothing at all," they agreed. "He just showed us a banana, it was in his trousers, but we didn't take it." The Nuns looked pleased and ordered the girls not to talk about him to anyone ever again, as it would frighten the little ones.

Corpus Christi was one of the loveliest days of the year. In the preceding days the children cleared the terrace and the avenue of any weeks or leaves. An Altar at the far end of the steps was decked in flowers under a beautiful canopy. The children took part in the procession that followed the Holy Monstrance, and attended with all the Nuns, Priests and altar boys as the Benediction was celebrated. Rose petals and flower petals were strewn in the path of the Eucharist. The singing was always very beautiful. The children were dressed all in white for the occasion. Afterwards the small children enjoyed collecting the petals to place and press in the pages of their prayer books. The scent of the petals and of the incense lingered for many hours and became part of the memory of Corpus Christi 'til the following year.

Mother Thérèse: First Mistress from 1940 was held in awe, fear and trepidation, as if she belonged in a celestial sphere. She had a conspicuous absence of compassion for the needs of some children. Yet, she singled out Elsie, and the children observed on an every day basis that their mistress was capable of responding with affection, especially to Elsie!

They were unable to perceive the reason in measures used, in correction, by their First Mistress. Her aim seemed to be "their submission". They were never to question, but to blindly trust.

Bedwetting was common among children up to twelve years and they were required to wear a distinguishing bonnet as a mark of disgrace! Noreen Quigley had her bed next to Frances's bed, just by the Visitors Stairs door, that led off the lower dormitory. That door, and the dormitory doors were locked at night. Quigley was a healthy looking child. She had a tremendous sense of humour, but she had a problem with her bowels! How she worried. She seemed to have no control in the situation. Every night she knelt by her bed for night prayers in unison, then delayed a minute longer while she said a special prayer, that she would not soil her bed that night! She had absolutely no way of knowing whether it would come away involuntarily or not! Some lucky mornings her bed was clean but on the unlucky mornings she was miserable and frightened. Maisie was a "help", who was also a "halfpenny short of a shilling"! She could wallop and lash out like a maniac when ordered to do so by Mother Thérèse. Frances, or any of the children had no idea where this crazy woman came from. She seemed to have been around since Noah! The children had a dread of Maisie. She was a middle-aged woman by 1945. She had two very short arms, one was even shorter than the other but those arms had strength in them. A blow from Maisie would render her opponent unconscious!

Noreen Quigley came under Maisie for punishment every time she soiled her bed. Maisie enjoyed to flog Noreen. Frances felt her pain with every lash. Frances tried prayer for Noreen's problem on a few occasions, deaf again - it seemed an epidemic of deafness in Heaven as far as Frances was concerned! Whatever would become of Noreen Quigley, Frances could not imagine. Noreen would try not to eat to prevent the mess, but eventually she gave in to hunger .... then the ultimate punishment!

Kathleen Boland's bed was situated on the far side of Frances's bed. Kathleen was a most attractive girl. Beautiful long slim fingers, with snow-white nails! She was probably desperately anaemic, but

Frances thought she looked divine. Kathleen was so sweet and very gentle. She too wanted to become a nun. Frances found it so difficult to understand the aim of her friends to want to spend their lives in any religious discipline after years of Mother Thérèse and Maisie! With Bunny's threat to become a nun, Kathleen Boland to follow, Kathleen Demond already gone to join a Convent, Joan Street determined to go to the Missions in Africa, all Frances ever really wanted was to own a sweet shop and to eat all her own sweets! Mary O'Rioden was already a nun in America. Frances was always aware of her teachers' help and guidance in education. Religious education worried her immensely. Her prayers were never answered. Mother Thérèse was quite wrong to say that Frances had a devil inside her.

The most disturbing fact that the child was expected to accept blindly, was that Jesus was born 1949 years ago. The world was millions of years old! What happened to good people before then, who were neither Protestant or Catholic? Why was it that everything she had to accept, and believe, happened tens of hundreds of years ago? Why couldn't God or Jesus just walk into the playroom, say hello everybody, I am Jesus, and just to prove it, do a miracle, or give Frances a glimpse of her Mother? No, faith again, excuses all the time. It would be no big deal, Frances thought, for God to just confirm a few points, just so people would agree and live in peace. There were too many mysteries, too many fairy stories. Frances loved the Chapel Architecture, the beautiful stained glass windows. The music - the words of some hymns were beautiful. She made up

134

her mind to accept all people, and to keep an open mind on all religions. To whomever made this wonderful world she was grateful. When old enough, she planned to investigate other religions. After all, she thought, the best way to prove a point was to try to disprove it. In the meantime she would listen and enjoy where it made sense. Time would tell the rest. Bunny disagreed absolutely. "It's a sin to disagree" she told Frances. Whatever "faith" was, Bunny had it. Frances did not have whatever it was that made believing so easy. She could not accept blindly. The Ten Commandments made some sense. It didn't matter to her who wrote them, they carried wisdom. They spelled out civilised behaviour. Whether God gave them to Moses, or the Old Man wrote them himself (he was missing long enough to do so) they were common sense rules for mankind.

Cork City is an historic area in the South of Eire. Its nucleus in the Sixth Century was the home of St. Finbarr and his fellow monks. They lived in the Gougone Barra region near Glengarrif. The valley is lonely and beautiful and the mountain scenery gazes down on to its lush green woods.

St. Finbarr became the first Bishop of Cork. With his monks and priests be built colleges, churches, and monasteries. Scenes of Glengarif and Gougone Barra are lush with green pastures. Wild fuchias and rhododendrons grow in profusion all along the route to Glengarrif. The shining lake in the valley houses a small island where St. Finbarr had his oratory in the Sixth Century. This holy social worker dedicated his life to the people of Cork. He ordained priests and educated the people to improve their standard of life, morally and spiritually. The Good Shepherd Nuns chose an apt name for their school at Sunday's Well, in Cork City, near the River Lee.

The magnificent Cathedral in Cork City, that serves the Cork citizens who follow the teaching of the Church of Ireland is exquisite to behold. Its great spires seem to touch the sky. It is built in Gothic style of the 13th Century France, by a convinced mediaevalist, William Burgess between 1867 and 1879, nine years after the opening of the Good Shepherd Convent.

Frances learned about Cork City in much detail from Mother Finbarr. The Shandon Bells captured the children's imagination and during the early years at St. Finbarr's when Cork City had much less traffic noise, the children could hear the sweet sound of the Bells as they played out the tune of the lovely words written by Father Prout who was born within their sound:

> "With deep affection and recollection
> I often think of those Shandon Bells.
> That sound so wild, would
> In days of childhood
> Fling round my cradle
> their magic spells.
> On this I ponder,
> Where'ere I wander,
> And thus grow fonder
> Sweet Cork of thee.
> For the Bells of Shandon,
> That sound so grand on -
> The pleasant water of the River Lee."

In common with all industrial schools in England and Ireland life was very restrictive for the children.

The nuns cared for large numbers of children from various backgrounds. Orphans, semi-orphans, abandoned, and children under- privileged and deprived. Compassion and paternalistic care was certainly the general policy of the dedicated nuns. Eighty two to one hundred and twenty children was not uncommon. They showed goodness and kindness to their unfortunate charges. The nuns moved steadily in care and education to help the children develop a normal life in a cloistered environment. they were motivated by a religious duty to God and Care. In the years from 1870 - 1957 girls only were accepted by the Good Shepherd Nuns.

Lack of training lay behind the kind efforts of the religious social workers. Their work policy lay submerged under an 1870 administrative procedure! Until the middle Fifties at best the nuns provided a sheltered life, safe from danger. A fair education to enable the girls to fit into society and employment. Tedium and lack of freedom restricted the children from meeting children in normal homes, visiting a cinema outside the convent grounds, having pets, to ride a bus, a train. Freedom to run about and to open doors instead of being locked in. To make a drink if needed, and to sit at any table of choice.

The nuns were not happy with their dilemma but could do little. Local authorities controlled the programme of care. The task of the good nuns would have been more difficult had it not been for the goodwill of the kind hearted people of Cork City, to enable the nuns to fulfil the standards required to help the defenceless children to achieve a place of worth in society.

CHAPTER TWELVE

Christmas 1949 was over and the new year began. Life with Mary and Bunny and Mother Coregia was happy and busy. Often the girls talked of the future. Frances pondered with a little fear, on what life would be like outside of the Convent life.

The three girls were of a similar age. There was no talk of careers. The girls just accepted whatever situation was found for them. Nursing had occurred to Frances. She was too young to train just then. She thought about England, especially of visiting Cheltenham and Oxford. She wondered if her father was still alive, and Aunt Mollie. They had all abandoned her. She wanted to visit them but she had forgotten addresses in nearly eleven years.

On a fine afternoon when all the bread was stacked on the shelves and the work for the day finished, the girls were chatting to Mother Coregia. There was a knock on the bakehouse front door, and immediately the door pushed open. the girls greeted Breda. She was a general help to Mother Thérèse, her appearance meant business. Mother Coregia looked towards Breda questioningly.

"Excuse me Mother," said Breda, "Mother Thérèse wants Frances, at once," she added. Frances looked towards Mother Coregia.

"Have you done anything wrong," asked the nun of Frances.

"No, nothing, but no doubt Mother Thérèse will know something," said Frances. Breda remained silent, although she must have known the situation.

Over many years, since Breda and Frances were six years old they enjoyed a friendly competitive relationship. Breda, for some reason known only to Mother Thérèse, went to town often. She visited her Aunt and Uncle in his tobacconist shop, and posted the mail at times. Although never a "snitch" she was never a special pal of anyone. In the Bakehouse that afternoon it seemed she knew nothing, saw nothing and heard nothing! Frances made the journey to the first dormitory floor, where Mother Thérèse gave Frances the news immediately.

"You are leaving us in one hour. Take a bath, put on the clothes that are on the chair in the bathroom. A General Costello will call for you and take you to Dublin." Frances was shattered by the news. She was speechless, she wanted to ask so many questions but couldn't communicate. She bathed quickly. She looked at the clothes on the chair. What was that, she picked up a bra, what was it, how does it go on? Panic turned to fear. Still shaken by the sudden news of leaving. She stood naked in the bathroom. She managed the panties. The bra and suspender belt were new to her. She had never seen anything like them in her life. She puzzled over the garments. Then her thoughts wandered to whatever would the outside world be like! Using money, she had no recollection of what it looked like! Mother Thérèse popped her head around the door, "Are you ready yet," she asked. She saw the bra in Frances's hand. She helped her on with the strange article of clothing, without a word, and left. Frances used her common sense to use the suspender belt. The stockings were thick horrible things, so strange. A pretty little dress that fitted nicely lifted her spirit momentarily. Mother Thérèse arrived with a hair brush. She brushed and brushed Frances's long red hair. Breda brought a pair of brown shoes, and encouraged Frances to wear them. A small suitcase was nearby. Mother Thérèse was putting some items into the suitcase and Frances looked at herself in the Bathroom mirror.

The dress was so pretty. She wondered if she would manage to take care of herself. How would she meet people. Would she ever see Bunny or Mary or Rosanna again. She was sad to be leaving, she knew so little about the outside world and her greatest fear was that of the unknown. It would be like being born at sixteen and a half years. The Parlour Nun arrived, dear lovely Mother Perpet, she hugged Frances and thanked her for all the work on the community staircase.

"Don't forget us," said the Nun. Frances couldn't answer, the words would not come.

"The car is here," the Parlour Nun called to Mother Thérèse. Quickly Mother Thérèse handed Frances a coat. It was too small for her, so Frances carried it. Then the Nun handed Frances fifteen shillings, and led the girl down the staircase, and through the hall to the Parlour. Mother Thérèse made no attempt to introduce the child and her employer.

General Costello was waiting in an adjoining room. Frances could hear his voice as the First Mistress bade him goodbye. He left to sit in his car and Mother Thérèse called for Frances. At last she spoke to the young girl.

"As I predicted, you are defiant to the end, every girl who leaves here cries, but not you," and with that

140

remark she slapped Frances's face for the last time, each side. Frances was filled with fear, and sick with loneliness, and confusion. The nun handed Frances her suitcase, just a tiny case. They walked out through the big oak door that she had entered through in 1939. The General stepped out to open the rear door for her. He shook hands with Frances and closed her door. She wondered what lay before her. She didn't notice the General returning to his seat, her head was spinning with fear of the unknown and of wild imaginings.

The engine put life into the huge sleek Limousine and she liked the sound of the wheels driving over the terrace gravel, that she and her young friends would never again walk on together. As the car drove down the avenue Mother Stanislaus was walking up and caught sight of Frances seated alone in the rear. Their eyes met for a fleeting moment, and a knife touched the child's heart. There wasn't even one second of time to say goodbye.

"How long have you lived here?" asked General Costello. Frances couldn't speak in her distressed state. He didn't ask again. Through the mirror he could see her in tears. The huge gates came into view and Frances saw the words in wrought iron. "Good Shepherd Convent". Over and over again she thought of the future and it was impossible to imagine. In all the years from six years old to sixteen and a half she had never seen the outside world. Nor held money, nor been inside a shop. The scenery took her mind off the worries. They were outside the city by the time Frances took notice of her surroundings. The General drove carefully in his splendid limousine. He was

Chairman of the Irish Sugar Beet Company of Ireland. He had ten children! On the journey they were to pick up one son from an Army base. The scenery was magnificent. Here and there Frances noticed the Celtic Crosses and Round Towers. She remembered learning from Mother Philomena that in olden days the Monks hid their manuscripts from the pagan evil hands of destruction. Cottages dotted about, some dilapidated, others picturesque. Old farmhouses, old ruins, old castles, run down villages and pretty villages. Old men sitting on low window sills chatting, a dog lazing in the sunshine by a house gate. The village shops with familiar names, O'Driscoll, McDonough, the pain of missing her friends of never saying goodbye, or knowing if they will ever meet again.

Mr Costello switched off the engine.

"I'll just be a few minutes," he called as he almost ran inside the high walled barracks. A sentry stood at the gate and Frances could see another soldier inside by an office window. He used a telephone, almost at once a young soldier joined the General. The two men chatted as they approached the car.

"This is Frances, she is coming to live with us to help mother," said the General to his son.

"My son," he said to Frances and both men settled in for the journey to Dublin. The car sped on swallowing the road. Fields on either side of wandering lanes. Through pine forests, through the beautiful village of Adare with its mediaeval castle and twelfth century cottages with thatched roofs. Skirting the Knockmealdown Mountains and on through Clonmel, through Kilkenny over the River

142

Barrow and the Town of Carlow. They crossed the River Slaney and approached the heavenly Wicklow Mountains. They kept left of the mountain range to enter Naas in County Kildare. Frances thought of Uncle Frank and if he ever gave her a thought. Darkness was near. The General switched on the car lights.

"We are driving through the Curragh now," he said, and Frances wanted to thank him for that information. Here in the Curragh her father had spent many of her young years and his. It was a panoramic carpet of green, so very beautiful. She could see how he or anyone could be very happy there. Frances longed for the journey to end, it had lasted five hours! How improper it would be, thought Frances, to ask the General to stop for the lavatory, or to venture to ask any question.

That sudden news of leaving! being wrenched from her friends and from the nuns she wanted to thank. She remembered her pigeon hole and its contents. A lovely picture given to her by Mother Finbarr on her Confirmation Day. A prayer book from Mother Brendan and pretty blue Rosary beads. Mother Thérèse gave her no chance to collect them. She planned to write and ask for them. If only she could get to a lavatory! Cars were coming from all directions and something she had never seen in her life, traffic lights!

"Another ten minutes," announced the General, "and we will be in Clontarf." Frances showed her interest at the kind gentleman's information by her expression. She could not utter a word. Along O'Connell Street, mental pictures from childhood were awakened. There it was, Dorset Place, she saw it, or maybe she didn't. They turned right by Parnell's statue and back down by the Gresham Hotel, and then turned left. Beautiful Georgian buildings with splendid doors, wide and full of character. They headed towards Fairview and on along the Clontarf Road and the sea wall that bounded Dublin Bay on the right. The car turned left into a tree-lined road.

"There," said the General, pointing to the house facing them at a 'T' junction, "is our house. The biggest in Clontarf at present." It was lit up and looked so warm and full of welcome. The tyres bounced up the driveway and stopped. Before Frances could greet Mrs. Costello who was standing in the doorway by the time she alighted, she asked the direction to the lavatory! Mrs Costello obliged instantly and took the small suitcase and waited in the hall for her. It was almost 10 p.m. For ten and a half years 7 p.m. was bedtime. Frances was utterly exhausted and bewildered.

"I'll show you to your room," said Mrs Costello. Children were running everywhere. There was one little girl and nine boys.

"Go to bed now," suggested Mrs. Costello, "and I'll meet you in the kitchen at 7.30 a.m." Frances took her little case and closed her bedroom door and locked it. She fell onto the bed and cried as though her heart would break. Where had the night gone? She awoke, fully dressed. What time was it? The children were running wild on the spacious landing and knocking on her door! What should I do? thought Frances . All her life she had woken to a bell, worked to order, now she had to think for herself. She removed her coat. She was pleased there was a wash basin in her room. She stripped and washed, and found an extra dress in her suitcase and an overall. She brushed her teeth and tidied her hair. She opened her bedroom door, and was besieged by lively children, all asking so many questions. On the way down to the kitchen with her new young friends she discovered it was only 6 a.m.! Mr. and Mrs. Costello were still asleep. The children wanted to show her everywhere, and Frances was terrified to venture into rooms beyond the kitchen until Mrs. Costello gave permission. They were beautiful children, and so lively. Frances had no idea of a normal home, or how children fitted in. She found bread and she toasted it for the children.

"We are twins," said Finbarr. Frances had no idea what twins were. A Martian landing on Dublin was the only comparison with Frances's experience of life outside an institution. She had acted always on orders. The children were giving her orders. Mrs. Costello arrived in her dressing gown. She was a tall heavy set lady with silver grey hair. Anyone, but Frances, would have considered Mrs. Costello too old for so many young children. Even the General was fifty-ish. Once the children were under control Mrs Costello took Frances on a tour of the house. Enormous rooms, beautifully furnished. There were so many rooms downstairs, and so many upstairs with bathrooms and lavatories. Beds to make, bathrooms to clean, washing and ironing, cooking for eleven, washing dishes, chickens to feed, children to mind, fires to light - no day would be long enough!

Three flights of stairs to clean! When Mrs Costello pointed out the Catholic church down on the Clontarf Road, Frances wondered how she would ever find time to go there! Mrs Costello was not in good health, and no matter how early Frances started in the morning, the day was never long enough! Her own room was at the top of the house. Many nights she was ironing and washing at midnight. Day after day she worked non-stop. There was no time for herself, it would have made an impossible situation even worse.

Frances loved the children, and the young ones had their meals in the kitchen, at a large table, with her. Mrs Costello told Frances to buy slippers, as soon as possible, as her heavy shoes were unsuitable for the carpet. There was no free time to travel to a shop, and even if there was time, Frances had no idea how to shop!

The days were forever, and the chores were endless. There was no washing machine. Tray cloths and tablecloths had to be starched and ironed. Fitting those tasks into keeping the house dusted and polished, with an eye on the clock to prepare vegetables and potatoes for lunch and for dinner. Mrs Costello was a busy lady on committees, and the telephone and doorbell were an extra burden. In all the years at the Convent the children never used a telephone. The Dublin accent was strange to her. Frances picked up the ringing telephone, and put it down again just to stop it ringing. She was the last person to bed at night, always after midnight. Mrs Costello filled an hot water bottle at 10 p.m. and reminded Frances of the priority tasks for the following day. For three weeks Frances tried to settle down. She still felt wrenched away from her friends. She could not bring herself to write to Mother Thérèse.

How can I ever take my half day, she thought. Who would do the work? She lay in bed with aching legs. Too tired to sleep. She glanced at a holy picture hanging over her bedroom door. The Costellos were Roman Catholics too. Frances stared at the picture, and the longer she stared the more angry she became at God, at Mother Thérèse, at her selfish father, wherever he was. If only she had the energy she would complain to Mother Thérèse about the job. Mrs Costello deserved better help than a sixteen and a half year old institutionalised Egit who couldn't use a telephone or communicate without feeling embarrassed. To not know anyone outside the Convent who could tell her about life? To know how to catch a bus, how to buy slippers and make up, and to apply the stuff! The more she thought the more she agonised. Where could she learn, where to begin, there was no time to learn. Then it came to her, run away, get out of that house with her fifteen shillings. She fell asleep. All next day she planned in her mind to leave early the next morning. She was into her fourth week. She worked hard all day and she felt sad and uneasy at leaving Mrs. Costello with all the work. The situation was impossible.

That night Frances took a piece of paper from the message pad, and in her room she wrote a note for Mr and Mrs Costello. She thanked them for their kindness and explained her reason for leaving, to find time to learn about life. She added that Mrs

Costello need not pay her, in view of leaving her with all the work. She placed the note on the table.

She thought of the lovely children, she knew how much work they created. Mrs Costello had loaned her an alarm clock and on that night she set it for 4 a.m. She took her bath, and went to bed. She lay there looking at the holy picture. Life was so frightening. She looked again at the picture and thought I won't ask God for help. He never answers me. She fell asleep.

The alarm woke her and in a sleepy confused move she sat up. She ran the tap quietly and washed as quickly as she could. She cleaned her teeth and dressed. All her belongings were in her small suitcase. She glanced around the small bedroom and aired the bed. The small window was always open. She held her shoes in one hand and the small suitcase in the other hand. She did not shut the bedroom door, the latch was a noisy one. Down the long carpeted staircase with its beautifully turned rungs and bannisters. Around and down the next flight of stairs. The hall clock just sounded the half hour. She hurried to open the front door. Two bolts to undo and she turned the door catch. She shut the door behind her gently. It was a chilly early morning. Her first walk on a Dublin Road. A long wide road led down to the sea front. Beautiful houses, enormous in size. Double fronted with fine carved front doors, with leaded and patterned fan lights. A milkman was busy. As Frances passed by he gave her a curious stare. She was numb with worry. Where to go, where to eat? Where to catch a bus into Dublin City? She reached the sea front. That early in the morning the area was like a ghost town. Frances sat on the sea wall to rest and to think. She felt helpless, as if deaf and blind. She rested her head in her hands. She didn't notice a policeman on duty walking towards her, on the grassy verge.

"What are ye doin' out at this early morning'? Frances almost slipped from the wall with fright. She looked at the officer, then stood up but couldn't answer for fear. She last saw a policeman at the children's court nearly eleven years ago on 28th October 1939. The officer sat on the wall and suggested that Frances should sit too.

"Tell me, where have you come from?" he asked in a kindly tone.

"From Mrs Costello's house at the top of the road," said Frances. "I couldn't do all the work by myself and I left this morning."

"Does Mrs Costello know you were worried?" he went on.

"No Sir, I thought she would send me back to the School in Cork and Mother Thérèse would tell everyone that I failed, she hates me."

"What School is that?" enquired the officer, as he beckoned Frances to sit on the sea wall beside him. She felt she could talk to him, there was an immediate rapport.

"The Good Shepherd Nuns looked after me since I was six years old. I was very happy there. I see now that my life will be difficult because I don't know anything about the world outside the Convent," said a tearful Frances. "I don't know the buses or how much to pay. I need slippers but I don't know if I have enough money or where the shops are. No one talks to me all day. The Costello children go to school." Frances felt she had lost all self respect. "I feel useless," she cried. "I know I have to work, everyone has to work, it is harder if you don't know how to answer a telephone. I feel I could do more in the house if I had more courage. I think I annoy Mrs Costello when I ask permission to do anything. In all my schooldays we had to ask for everything, or wait to be told or wait for the bell to ring. I feel as if I can only live and work under orders. I'm afraid to think for myself." She had so much to say and the kind policeman listened attentively.

"Did you ever hear of the Legion of Mary?" he asked.

"Yes, I knew about them, Mother Brendan told us about their work," said Frances feeling pleased that she knew something. "Well, my wife is one, and I am sure that she will help you, some way," he said. "But first, let us go along to the station nearby, and get a cup of tea and take a few notes and see what can be done."

"What station, Sir, I won't go on any train," Frances was upset again.

"No, no, the Gárda Station," said the officer, as he steered the young girl in the direction. On the way to the station the policeman talked of jobs with other girls until she got used to "the ways".

"I know the Nuns are good people and where would we be without them," he said. "The rules are hard for them too. Time will come when children will be less institutionalised. Then they'll have more confidence. Right now you feel stupid and useless, but you are better educated than many girls walking

150

about. When you get confidence you will be grand. We have a boys school here called Artane, and I see those kids, and how they struggle to fit into society when they leave, because they all lack confidence in any challenge. Same as you, but you'll be alright. The Legion ladies know everyone," he added. They had been walking along the sea front wall, and now they crossed the road to a small Gárda Station. The Gárda ushered Frances in ahead of him. The Station Gárda looked up

"What have we got here," he said looking at Frances.

"Oh, this young lady is lost in Dublin. I'm going to make a call for help, but I'll make a cup of tea first," said Frances's new friend. "Give your name and address to the Gárda there, give the Costello's address, only for records," encouraged the kind Gárda. Frances was bewildered and worried, the experienced eye of the Gárda observed that.

"Do you take sugar," he asked.

"I don't know, thank you, I'm not sure if we had sugar in our tea."

"'Tis sugar then," replied the officer. "You'll need that today."

CHAPTER THIRTEEN

A short walk from the station led them to a terraced house. A neat and tidy garden surrounded by a white wooden fence. A tap on the window, announced their arrival, and his wife opened the door. She greeted Frances warmly, and took her small case.

"Leave it here for a while, and come on into the kitchen, and have a cup of tea, and maybe some toast, would you like that?" asked the very kind and friendly lady. Frances thanked her, and said that she had no wish to trouble the family. She expressed her sincere gratitude to the Police Officer,

"Sure, he's doing this all the time, he loves to help people" said his wife with a smile. "I'll leave you now to work out something," the Gárda said, as he climbed the stairs. "Good luck now," he said to Frances and she thanked him again. A young lady appeared at the kitchen door. "Oh, this is Eileen, our daughter. Eileen this is Frances," said the Gárda's wife. Eileen extended her hand to Frances and replied with a warm "hello". Frances greeted the young girl and apologised for disturbing the family. "Don't mention it," said Eileen, "Mammy enjoys to help, she loves the Legion and it keeps her happy. I'm off to work now, I must hurry or I'll miss the bus." She called cheerio to her father and shut the front door behind her. The two ladies sat in the kitchen. It was warm and cosy with a smell of toast. Mary opened the conversation,

"Sean must have faith in you, he told me on the 'phone about your problem. He feels that you should be with other young girls, to help you around, and I was wondering if I 'phoned the supervisor at the Mater Hospital where they are always ready to take on help." Frances listened attentively and felt joy at every word.

"I'm sure I would be able to do that work, with others, and I would do my best," said Frances eagerly.

"I don't know your name," said Frances.

"Ah, 'tis Mary, Mary Tierney. Sean is my husband."

"Thank you, Mrs Tierney," said Frances with a smile, "you are the first person I've talked to other than Mrs Costello."

"Call me Mary," said Frances's new friend. "Finish your toast, then freshen up when the bathroom is empty, and leave your case here today, we'll be back. We will take the bus to Eccles Street to the Mater Hospital. My friend works there in Personnel. She belongs to the Legion of Mary. She may be able to fix up some work, we'll try anyway," said Mary, while Frances hung on to her every word.

"I'm so grateful to you, really," said Frances. "I had no idea what to do, or where to begin, and I didn't want to let the nuns down, I really couldn't cope," Frances added.

"Now, listen," said Mary, "Many boys leave "Artane", here in Dublin, frightened, with no confidence. At times, Sean's colleague has helped them, they just need a push in the right direction. Plenty are waiting to exploit them. They are so naïve and the City is so dangerous. We often talk about children and young people in need of 'after care help' there is none, except whatever the Legion of Mary and others can do, that is, whenever we hear of a case," said Mary with a concerned look.

"Were you happy at the school," asked Mary.

"Yes, I was, I suppose," said Frances. "I miss my friends very much. The nuns too. They taught me a great deal, and I will always be grateful to them. I wasn't an angel, I got a few wallops, but if the First Mistress didn't care she probably wouldn't have tried so hard with me. You know, Mary, I often used to wonder why she picked up the cane so often to me. I would have been pleased to just have a little praise from her, I would have been good for her then. She was so hurtful with her words, it didn't give me the heart to want to please her, but my teachers were so kind and so, so, well, real nuns, so gentle. I know I will never forget them, and all they did for me. I want to do well, if only to prove the First Mistress wrong about me," said Frances.

"Well, you are half way there already, you have the will, and the purpose, you just need the opportunity, eh," said Mary. "Well let's find that opportunity," Mary encouraged. "The bathroom is free now, Frances, and I'll 'phone Personnel at the hospital," said Mary.

Within twenty minutes Mary and Frances were on the bus to O'Connell Street, Frances observed how Mary stated her destination, and the conductor mentioned the fare. The two friends chatted on the bus journey, and Frances showed a keen interest in the areas on route to Dublin City.

Malahide was signposted to the right, and Howth, she remembered seeing those signs from General Costello's car. They journeyed by shopping scenes, schools, "Public House", she read over the long glazed building.

"What happens in there?" she asked Mary.

"Oh, that's a bar, the less you see of the inside of that place the safer you'll be," said Mary with a smile. "Men drink Guinness and whiskey in there. There was a time when women would never go to a pub or a bar, but they do now."

"Oh, yes," said Frances, "I remember Mother Clotilde telling us about the problems of drink."

"The drink can ruin family life," said Mary, "and many good women are left alone to bring up their children when their man is an alcoholic," added Mary. The busy traffic and the extra crowds of people was one sure sign that they were approaching the City. They passed Amien Street Station, and Frances wondered if that was the station she and Kathleen left from in 1939 to travel to Cork. It all seemed so long ago. She fought her fears of the unknown that morning by pretending all was well. But as an adult she could not play games for long. She had to face reality. Suddenly, a man jumped on to the bus as it slowed down.

He instantly shouted "Bang bang, bang bang," and ran upstairs. Everyone laughed and chatted about him. Frances got such a fright. She looked at Mary who was laughing so much.

"Who is it?" asked a half scared, half smiling Frances. Mary recovered her composure,

"'Tis only 'Bang-Bang'," she replied. "He's not right in the head, and he goes up and down the streets, on and off buses, in and outa shops, shouting 'bang bang!' everyone knows him, he's harmless, but he would frighten you the first time," said Mary. "Come, this is our stop."

They walked around a corner to O'Connell Street, a wide thoroughfare. A sea of people hurrying to and fro. They had to catch another bus to Eccles Street. They walked past ice-cream parlours and crossed over to the Metropole Cinema, where they boarded a waiting bus. Frances observed the numbers on the bus stop. She felt so excited. She was grateful to Mary. She had to say so, and Mary only waved a hand saying,

"I know you are worth helping. My husband could see that too. Maybe one day you will do the same for someone in need." Frances remembered the headline in her transcription book many years before, "A friend in need is a friend indeed". Mary pointed to the General Post Office, a well known historic building on the left, and across the road the Gresham Hotel, that catered for film stars and many famous people. Cleary's, the huge store that looked like fairyland at Christmas time and over on the left a large Maternity Hospital, "the Rotundra," said Mary. Frances wanted to know what Maternity Hospitals were for. She passed the next ten minutes mulling over the word 'maternity' in her mind, and decided it had to relate to 'mother, somehow. She decided against asking Mary for an explanation, another time maybe. They reached the Mater Hospital. The bus almost emptied. Mary explained to Frances that the passengers were likely to be patients and may be staff. Visitors were more likely to be on the evening bus.

Inside the building nurses hurried about, porters pushed chairs and trolleys. There were nuns, too, who appeared to work there. Domestic workers polished already gleaming floors.

"Now," said Mary, "accept any job you are offered, to get a start. They have staff accommodation and when you get your feet firmly on the ground you could look for a better job. Many girls go to England to train in nursing. You can do that if you feel you could manage the studying. Have you got your School Leaving Certificate? she asked Frances.

"Yes, I have it in the suitcase, said Frances.

"Well, you are not old enough for another six months. By then you should have enough confidence to do whatever you wish. The student nurses here receive no salary, they have to be supported by their family. In England they pay the student nurses, not much, but it gets them through their three and a half years training. A lot of girls go over, it's a pity for Ireland. In time I suppose it will improve here. Our economy is not as good as England's. One day we'll make it," said Mary, with pride in her voice.

They reached the Personnel Office, and a middle-aged lady greeted Mary warmly.

"This is Frances," said Mary. The lady smiled a welcome, and offered them a seat.

"I have an application form here, so if Frances would fill it out and sign the bottom while I go to talk to the Administrator and see if she needs help, I believe her girl is off sick." Mary looked pleased and that gave Frances some confidence.

"She is really nice," said Frances.

"She's in the Legion, too," answered Mary, "We often work together," she added.

Frances filled in the form and for her home address Mary kindly suggested that Frances could use hers. Frances thanked Mary and wondered how she could ever repay Mary's kindness. The Personnel lady returned.

"We're OK, Frances will work in the office until their girl comes back, then we'll find her something else. She can live in and we'll pay her 12/6d a month, and all her food. When can she start?" asked the Personnel lady. Mary glanced at Frances and asked,

"Tomorrow?"

"Yes, tomorrow and thank you," said Frances looking at the hospital officer and at Mary in turn.

"Thanks a million," said Mary to the Personnel friend, and Frances could detect that the two ladies found satisfaction in helping her.

"Call to this office at 8.30 a.m., and I'll get you fixed up with cards and an overall, and don't be late," said the lady. Mary and Frances walked happily to the exit. Frances asked Mary about accommodation for that night.

"Oh, stay with us, silly," said Mary with a smile. "Sean will be delighted for you," she went on.

"I can't believe that I have a job and that I can live in, it is a load off my mind, and all thanks to you, Mary, and to Mr Tierney. One day, maybe, I will prove my gratitude to you both," said Frances.

"Write to the nuns," encouraged Mary. "They must be worried about you."

"Mrs Costello must have 'phoned them," said Frances, "and I am sure that only Mother Thérèse would know, and she won't care a dot about me. When I'm getting on well I'll write, I promise," said Frances.

While waiting at the bus stop, Mary used every minute to advise.

"Frances, don't be afraid of anyone. Keep your personal information to yourself. Learn all you can, and in six month's time if you would like to train in nursing, let us know and we will put you in touch with an English hospital. I think you would like that work," said Mary.

The bus arrived and Mary prompted Frances to ask for "two to the Pillar". Frances felt she was taking her first steps in her new life. The worry had weighed heavily. It seemed an age since 4 a.m. that morning. Had her Guardian Angel sent that Gárda to her aid!

Frances remembered that she had 15/- and it was in her pocket. She had no purse or handbag. She offered Mary the money.

"Please Mary, take it for all the fares and expenses."

"No, no, no," Mary looked horrified. "Frances, we are happy to help you, and if you want to show us your gratitude, then do well, and remember that to get anything out of life you have to put something into life. You are alone, I know, but you are young and intelligent and healthy. Take one day at a time. You'll get there," said Mary. They reached the Pillar. "We'll just nip into Moore Street and get some vegetables and a bit of meat for this evening," said Mary.

"Oh, Mary, I don't eat meat," said Frances.

"Are you vegetarian," asked Mary.

"If that means no meat, then I am that!" said Frances, "especially black pudding and all the lumps of fat!" laughed Frances.

They passed the GPO. It looked enormous. Frances glanced up at its huge heavy pillars.

"That was the 1916-21 Headquarters," said Mary, "where the freedom fighters fought and died. And we're still not free!" said Mary. Frances remembered Mother Bridget's lessons and how they learned that the temporary government was set up, and a Constitution was signed by a group of Patriots, she could only remember Thomas MacDonough. Moore Street was a scene to behold.

"Tuppence each the ripe bananas," yelled a big-bellied woman, with greasy hair and a few dirty brown teeth. Most of the teeth were missing. Barrow after barrow of beautiful fruit and fresh vegetables. Barrows of fresh flowers. Every seller shouted his wares as if to drown the voice of his and her comrades. Beautiful babies and tots near the barrow owners, strapped safely in prams. Newspaper sellers screaming out 'Irish Independent'" some as young as ten years old. The ground littered with fruit boxes and scraps of tissue papers in green, that once wrapped oranges or apples.

"Here yar love, taste it," said a seller as she thrust a filthy dirty hand that held a piece of orange to Frances.

"Take it," nudged Mary laughing, "don't eat it though."

"Thank you," said Frances to the fruit seller.

"God bless you love," came the reply. Mary stopped to buy some vegetables while Frances observed the seller, whose lovely features were tired looking, and her poor hands showed signs of hard work. The child in the pram beside her looked healthy and happy. Again Frances remembered a line from her school book "'Tis honest toil, that does no man wrong." They moved on.

They passed Woolworths. Suddenly Frances remembered a scene that took place in that very shop in 1938. She screamed and kicked and lay on the saw-dusted floor, aged five years, because her mother would not buy her a 'Shirley Temple' lollipop! The truth was now clear to Frances, her poor mother could not afford the huge lollipop, that was then a new rage from Hollywood. Frances followed Mary, and enjoyed the market scene. It was an interesting lesson in shopping. Mary and Frances walked to O'Connell Street and towards the direction of the bus queue for Clontarf. There was a heavy crowd waiting for the bus. Everyone waited patiently. The Clontarf bus pulled around from O'Connell Street and the queue surged forward. Stepping up on to the platform Frances collided gently with another passenger, she instantly apologised and glanced at her victim.

"Tessie! Tessie O'Keefe!" Both girls were amazed to see each other.

"Frances, when did you leave?" asked Tessie.

"Push down now, please," called the busy conductor. Mary was as excited as were the girls. All three had to stand inside, they didn't mind standing, at least they got on and were moving.

"Mary, this is Tessie, she was at school with me, she left about a year ago, we were always good friends," said Frances.

"Wonderful," said Mary, "now you have a friend." Tessie was a very attractive girl from Limerick who had spent eleven years at Sunday's Well School. The girls had too much to talk about and no time to say much.

"Take my telephone number," said Tessie "'Phone me soon, and we'll fix up to meet. My day off is Thursday," Tessie added. "Where do you work?" she asked Frances, but before Frances could explain Mary rang the bell. Their stop was next. The girls were delighted to have met and Frances promised to 'phone. Tessie's face was a delight. She was always a good friend at school. Mother Thérèse had a difficult time correcting Tessie's bad temper. Mary and Frances alighted and Frances clutched the piece of paper with her school friend's telephone number. As the bus moved off they waved to Tessie.

"How fortunate that you met your friend," said Mary. "In time you will probably meet others," Mary said.

When they arrived at Mary's house, Gárda Tierney was asleep upstairs. He was on night shift that week. They moved about quietly. Mary put the kettle on.

"Give Tessie another half hour to get in, Frances, then 'phone her," encouraged Mary. Frances offered to do some housework, it seemed the least she might do, and it would help to pass the afternoon. Mary gratefully accepted her help. Together, they thoroughly cleaned the sitting room and the windows inside and outside. They couldn't "do" the stairs or any upstairs rooms in case they disturbed the sleeping Gárda. Mary discussed his job, and told Frances that the pay was not good. In England he would earn a lot more, said his loyal wife. Sean took his job very seriously and worried about the crime rate.

Frances 'phoned Tessie on the 'phone in the hall, a heavy black instrument with a dial that sounded too loud, Frances was afraid of disturbing Mr Tierney. Mary had given her a lesson on using the telephone. Tessie answered almost immediately. Frances explained very quickly that the past month had been hell for her but that was a story for when they met. "Mrs Costello?" asked Tessie, "that's the fellow that heads the sugar beet. So you were in CLONTARF," said Tessie, "so is your sister, Kathleen."

"What! Kathleen is here too?" asked Frances, keeping her voice rather quiet. Frances couldn't believe her ears. "Tess, let's meet on Thursday of next week, because this week is difficult for me," said Frances. "OK," agreed Tessie.

"I'll 'phone you again," promised Frances.

"Don't forget now," asked Tessie.

"I won't forget," Frances promised laughingly. "Bye, bye for now!" said Tess.

Frances returned to Mary who was preparing vegetables in the kitchen. She picked up a knife to help. Mary switched on a radio but kept the sound down. Frances again thanked Mary for her kindness. She offered Mary her 15/-. Mary emphasised that she would need that money herself as the hospital may not pay her for the first month. The two friends passed a very happy hour preparing the dinner. Eileen usually got home about 6 p.m. She worked for the Posts and Telegraph office. Mary spoke very highly of her daughter. They would have liked more children but it was not to be. Frances was as innocent as any child of six on matters relating to sexual behaviour and pregnancy and childbirth. The teachers had never touched on that subject. However, what she didn't know didn't worry her. The only time she had felt confused, on such an issue, was when Mrs Costello told her that the twins, who were nine years old, affected her health because they "arrived" so late. Frances assumed that the twins were late coming home one night and Mrs Costello was worried sick! Mary had no idea of Frances's lack of knowledge and she chatted away about Eileen's birth. Most of the conversation was way over Frances's head.

Eventually Mr Tierney came down to join them. He looked fresh and neat. He had slept well. He wanted to know the day's news. He was very pleased to hear about the new job and accommodation. Frances gained enough confidence to talk to her new friends. She expressed her gratitude to Mr Tierney for his help.

"Don't mention it," said the Gárda, "you are on the right road now, and it is all up to you now whether you do well or not," he continued. Eileen arrived and asked about the job. Everyone was happy and they all sat down to dinner. Frances observed family life. She was grateful to the Tierney family, and she told them so at the table. The Gárda asked many questions about her life in Sunday's Well. He seemed very interested in the way the nuns managed to cope with so many children. He believed that much would be changed if only the nuns had more 'say'. He had an interest in the children at Artane Boys School in Dublin. He felt that the Government would do more to help the children when the economy improved, that the nuns and Christian Brothers were far from satisfied with the limitations imposed on them by the bureaucracy.

"In time," said the Gárda, "children in need will take their place in City schools, they will be housed in small groups, and that the creative thoughts of humanitarians would be effective. Positive steps would be taken on a large scale, to provide supportive care, within the family, rather than seeking to improve the care given to children when they became deprived."

Frances agreed that it would be better for the children if the family could be helped in times of crisis, which would, in the long run, be more satisfactory than separating the child. In her own case she could see that the court had no alternative but to rely on the nuns. The sisters who dedicated their lives to the case of the helpless and the needy deserved recognition. The nuns were substitute parents, and their kindness and interest in he children helped them to grow emotionally and physically, and in most cases the children came to terms with their environment. Frances felt that her emotional needs were more than catered for. The First Mistress had tremendous responsibility, and that lady may not have been the best choice for the position she held. She was artistic and super-sensitive. She seemed to have needs of her own. The sheer number of children made the situation very difficult for the mistress to consider the individual needs of every child. With all the School's teachers Frances felt she had developed an affectionate relationship. She believed that she had found stability, and that the wonderful nuns had provided warmth and understanding. Frances was grateful for a sound and useful education. The nuns did their best in the circumstances. Children were placed under their care for ten or more years. Whatever their personality, conduct, intellectual capacity, emotional state or social history, the nuns had to find a way to cope. To attend to each child's needs would involve a whole series of specialised services. The nuns were in a position to provide only a shelter, a general standard of living, health precautions, and a level of education that would enable the young adult to fit into society. Millions of children in normal homes received no more advantages, and many received even less. Vocational guidance and the use of leisure time were situations that Frances had to work out for herself. The position with the Costellos was absolutely unsuitable for her, and sadly, when Frances left the School the First Mistress did not help her to feel that in any difficulty, she could see further advice or help from the nun. In fairness, Frances had to admit that in view of the personality clash between herself and that single nun, who was the only nun she could have sought help from, she would have died rather than seek help from the First Mistress. Fortunately, Gárda Tierney saved her future. The majority of children found a way to keep peace and pace with Mother Thérèse. Therefore much of the struggle that Frances experienced had to be partly of her own making. She recognised that fact, she simply could not deal with it. Maybe in time.

The discussion in association was indeed therapeutic. The Tierneys were excellent parents and Eileen had benefited greatly from their wisdom and understanding.

Gárda Tierney left for night duty, and wished Frances success. She would have left next morning by the time he arrived home. Eileen had to go to a

Sodality Night. Frances had no idea what that meant. It became just another "wonder what that is" in Frances's mind. In time, she thought, she would catch up with everyone. Mary and Frances washed up after dinner. They settled down to a nice cup of tea and applecake.

"I enjoyed our discussion," said Frances. "How helpful that would have been in school, if we met every Sunday, or whenever, and each child encouraged to talk out her fears and ideas. Instead, we listened, or didn't listen, to the First Mistress going on and on about what God expects and what God wants. What about my wants!" laughed Frances. Mary who was deeply religious, didn't smile.

"Be careful, Frances, of your religion. It is the most important foundation in your life. Without religion you have no worthwhile purpose in your life."

"You are quite right," said Frances with respect, but deep down she felt she had a point of her own. The religious rules were all very well in moderation, but there were such needs as her own. If they had meetings in school, even in the young classes, pent up feeling would have been released. There would have been an opportunity for the children to have their lack of confidence restored. It would have corrected a great weakness that comes from being forced to accept adult opinion as dogma. Perhaps Frances would have discovered where she and Mother Thérèse crossed swords. Mary noticed Frances was deep in thought.

"A penny for them," said Mary smiling.

"For what?" asked Frances. Mary laughed,

"You were deep in thought, and so we say 'a penny

for them' - that means tell me what you are thinking about," said Mary. Frances was amazed,

"I have so much to learn, Mary, I feel I am on some foreign shore and that I have to learn the language, and the rules," said Frances with a worried look.

"You'll pick up everything in no time," said Mary. "Oh, you'll meet so many types of people. You'll have to discover the lazy one who will land you with most of the work. The spender who will ask you for money, and never give it back, so be careful. The gossips, have nothing to do with them. Don't pick up swear words." Frances interrupted,

"Swear words?" Mary smiled,

"Yes, there are plenty, you will hear them, but don't use them."

"I thought 'swear' meant on the Bible, in court," said Frances giggling.

"Well, Frances, bad language is probably a better description."

"How will I know the difference?" asked Frances.

"You'll realise it from the content of the sentence," said Mary. "Tessie will probably tell you all about that, she has been here a year now, and she will be able to enlighten you."

The two friends talked until late. Eileen arrived about 10.30 p.m, tired and made a cup of tea for all and bade them goodnight. She asked Frances if she would like to take the same bus into town with her, as she had to go into Dublin too, every morning. Frances was very happy to accept, and said so. Mary tried to give Frances as much advice as possible, and Frances again thanked her for all the help.

"Keep in touch," said Mary warmly. "I hope Tessie will prove to be a good friend. If you discover she is different, keep a wise head. We are always here if you have a serious problem," said Mary.

"Mary, whatever happens in my life, wherever I go, and no matter how old I become, I will remember that you and your husband among the lovely nuns, were my compass. I have tons to learn, and I will make mistakes, but the thought of you and Sean and Eileen and the nuns will knock me back on to the difficult but correct path," said Frances in tears. Mary cried too. Then said Mary,

"We mustn't wallow!"

"Wallow?", and they both laughed again. "Mary, will I ever know life outside?" asked Frances.

"Yes you will in no time," encouraged Mary as they climbed the stairs to their rooms.

CHAPTER FOURTEEN

Frances was in good time for work. She was allocated to the Admin Office for four weeks. There were some other girls and young men who greeted her and introduced themselves and one of the girls came from Cork City. She filed away paperwork and ran errands to other offices. The Mater Hospital was very large and Frances soon learned where the wards were and the various departments. She felt very happy and enjoyed the hospital environment. She worked until 5.30 p.m. and went to her room on a corridor where other staff had accommodation. Many went home at weekends, she learned from snippets of conversation. Frances 'phoned Tessie and agreed to meet her on Thursday at 6 p.m. at the Metropole. Tessie was delighted to meet her. They went inside the Metropole for tea. Tessie knew one of the waiters. She met him at a dance hall. He would serve them, and not charge them, said Tessie. Frances was too naïve to understand the perks of friendships. She was so happy to be with Tessie. The restaurant was the first in Frances's life. She looked around in awe. The young waiter approached them. Tessie introduced Frances.

"My boss is watching me," said the waiter, "so just give me your order. We'll talk later," he said.

"Bring tea and a selection of cakes, please," said Tessie. The waiter winked at Frances and Tessie told Frances that he was a bit of an ejit but very handy for afternoon tea! Frances laughed nervously and pitied the poor lad. Tessie asked about Frances's job, and when and how she left Sunday's Well. It was a long story and Tessie agreed that the Tierney's were saints! Tessie worked for a family as a children's nurse in Baggots Street. They had a chemist shop. The boss was the Pharmacist and the wife ran the business. Tessie was very happy there.

"Your sister, Kathleen, is out in CLONTARF at Hollybrook Road. She minds two children. She wants to leave for England. Maybe you could take her job. That way we could have our half days off together. I get off at 1 p.m. every Thursday. I'll give you Kathleen's telephone number and you can 'phone from here. Finish your tea first," said Tessie. The waiter kept coming over to them and Tessie was tired of him but she had to be nice to him to avoid the bill. She made some remark about seeing him later in the 'Galway Arms' dance hall and he seemed delighted. They left the restaurant and used the 'phone downstairs. It was out of order, so they walked up to the GPO. Tessie knew Dublin very well. A whole line of 'phones, Frances was amazed. Tessie showed her how to make a call from a public 'phone. "Press Button A, then speak". Kathleen was surprised to hear from her. After the initial surprise, Kathleen asked her to meet later that evening. Tessie and Frances walked up and down O'Connell Street. They had so much to talk about.

The time went by so quickly. Kathleen arrived on time. The two sisters were still strangers. It had always been that way. There was no chemistry at all. They were pleased to know where each one was, and Kathleen explained her job. It was in a smallish, end of terrace house. She kept the house clean and tidy, and looked after two young children, Deirdre and Ronan. She was happy there, but felt old enough to go to England, and earn more money. She had secured herself a nice job in Lancashire but couldn't let the children down, she needed someone suitable. She then asked Frances to leave the job at the Mater and take over her job. Frances was unable to think for herself, it was a weakness, that in time she hoped to control.

"How do I do that?" asked Frances. "Go to the Personnel Office and tell them that you would like to leave, that you found a job with your sister. They won't mind at all," said Kathleen. "Come out now and meet Mr. and Mrs Woods," urged Kathleen. Frances felt uneasy, and wanted to say so. She had no courage, little confidence and certainly she could not say no. In her mind she became confused again. She was settled, she was content, and now another new beginning. Tessie felt that until she was older, she was better in a job such as Kathleen's. They walked up Hollybrook Road to Mrs. Woods.

The children were delightful. The little boy was fourteen months, and the little girl was four years old. Frances agreed to take the job just to satisfy

Kathleen. The pay was lower than the Hospital. Tessie told Frances that she would meet her every Thursday at 2 p.m. There was no debate. Frances accepted the job and promised to telephone to confirm her starting date.

Next morning Frances went to see the lady in Personnel who so kindly gave her the job. The lady wished her well.

"Come back any time if you want work," she kindly added. Frances was not happy to leave but remembered something Tessie had said,

"You are not street-wise enough to work in a hospital," whatever that meant. Sunday was the day to start with the Woods, and Frances 'phoned to confirm that. Kathleen left for England the day before without a word of goodbye to her sister. It didn't affect the younger sister. They had never been like real sisters. Kathleen left for England and out of her sister's life.

Deirdre and Ronan were delightful to look after. On Frances's first evening she learned the physical difference between a girl and a boy, at the childrens' bathtime. She was not disturbed, just took it all in her stride. She was aware that there was much to learn. Mrs Woods had a great sense of humour and in that way she helped Frances. She also gave Frances magazines to read. Life was much easier than at the Costello's. Deirdre started school in September at the Dominican Convent in Eccles Street and every morning Mrs Woods took the little girl to school on the bus. Mr Woods took the family car to his office in Dublin. He was an extremely nice man. He was a Director in a corset factory. Frances remained behind to look after the little boy and to do the housework. Ronan was a most contented little one. He played quietly for hours in his playpen. Mrs Woods brought home fresh vegetables and other ingredients and prepared and cooked lunch for everyone. Mr Woods always came home for lunch. They were a very happy family. Later in the day Mrs Woods set off to collect Deirdre from school. After dinner every evening

Frances would iron the children's clothes, and wash her own clothes. They had no washing machine and no hoover in those early months. Frances attended to Ronan mostly, Mrs Woods looked after Deirdre.

She was an excellent mother. Her children were very important to her. She dressed them well. All their little shirts and dresses were made by a dressmaker who lived on the next road. The house was small by Clontarf standard in 1950/51. It was so easy to keep it clean and tidy. Ronan was Frances's sole charge and she adored him. The grandparents were always very welcome. Mrs Woods's mother, Mrs Murphy, had a cardiac problem and at times the daughter would bring her mother to Hollybrook Road and no matter how disorganised life became, for two or three weeks, Mrs Woods cared for her mother with great love. Frances observed and learned a great deal from her employer's way of life.

Mrs Woods's father had already died before Frances joined them. Mrs Woods referred lovingly to him as 'Ahair' She loved the Gaelic language and could speak fluently with her brothers whenever they visited. Brendan in particular was fluent in Gaelic.

Her younger brother was a Priest. Father Murphy visited from time to time. He had a Country Parish. Mr Woods's lovely parents visited too, and often came to dinner. Mrs Woods was an excellent cook. She took great pride in laying a perfect table. Frances enjoyed helping and learning. The silverware was cleaned to a brilliant shine. Organisation and method was the key to success at any dinner party. It paid off, those evenings were a great success. Frances met Tessie every Thursday and she was learning so much about life. She was happy with Mrs Woods.

That summer the family went away to an hotel for a break. Frances remained behind, alone. She kept busy and answered the telephone and took her half days off as usual and in no time the family returned. Ronan was so excited to see her. They had a family pet dog called Bran who lived in a purpose-built kennel in the garden. He was a cocker spaniel, absolutely adorable. The children could do anything with him, even sat on his back. He was such a good natured little dog.

One Saturday after they returned from holidays, Bran got out, somehow, and ran on to the road. Frances couldn't leave Ronan who was by then only two years old. That evening Mr and Mrs Woods went down to the sea front to look for him, and found him lying dead on the grass verge. Deirdre who was nearly five years old was inconsolable. The local chemist had heard the screech of brakes and ran out to the badly injured dog. Seeing how much pain he had to be in, he put chloroform over his face until he died. Mr Woods buried the pet by the sea wall.

Frances kept in touch with Mary, Sean and Eileen and they were very interested in her progress. Frances could not bring herself to write to Mother Thérèse. Christmas 1950 was a very happy one and Frances wanted to train to be a nurse but was loathe to leave Ronan.

In the summer of 1951, the Woods took a large house in Skerries for two weeks. The children were so excited to have Frances on holiday with them. Ronan was very attached to her. Skerries was a lively holiday resort. Funfairs, sailing boats and donkey rides, a wonderful atmosphere.

Tessie 'phoned with devastating news that she was moving to England with her job. The chemist and his wife and family were taking her with them. She promised to write and let Frances know about life over there. Although Frances loved the children she knew she, too, had to leave for some training. She couldn't spend her life with Mrs Woods. She was at a crossroads and she planned to talk to Mary and Sean. Although the family were on holiday, the children had to be in bed at the normal time of 7 p.m. Mr and Mrs Woods went out most evenings with visitors. One evening a visitor left an evening paper in the lounge and Frances looked through the pages while the little ones slept. Then her eye fell on an advertisement for Student Nurse applicants - "Girls from 18 required to train in Nursing". Frances got her pen and paper and applied. She felt the time was right. She posted it next morning. She explained in her letter that the address given would be used until the 31st then she referred the answer to Hollybrook Road.

Within a week she received a reply and an appointment for an interview at the Shelbourne Hotel in Dublin within four days. Frances asked for time to go to Dublin on the date stated and Mrs Woods agreed. She wanted Frances back at Skerries by 6 p.m. Seemed easy enough at the time. Mrs Woods took over the care of Ronan that day. Her appointment was for 11.15 a.m. She got there in good time and found that the interviews were running fifteen minutes late. At last she was called and met a charming lady. Frances produced her School Leaving

Certificate. However, the lady insisted on giving her a test by the General Nursing Council for England and Wales. Many questions were asked and Frances answered happily.

"You may take this as confirmation of our acceptance," smiled the lady interviewer. "Please arrive by 2nd September. Frances thanked her and left. She took a bus to O'Connell Street and posted a card to Mary and Sean and Eileen with the news. She bought some shoes and little pieces, shampoo and toothpaste and caught the bus to Skerries. With the interviews running late and the break for lunch hour, then her shopping, time was nearly 4 p.m. Traffic had built up and on route towards the airport Frances worried about the time. The driver seemed to be in no hurry. Eventually the bus pulled into Skerries after 6 p.m. Mr and Mrs Woods had already left and a guest was baby-sitting until France returned. She apologised and had a feeling that she was in serious trouble. She went to the children's bedroom. Deirdre was already bathed and Frances prepared the bath for Ronan.

"Are you leaving us," asked Deirdre. Frances was surprised at the question.

"Well, very soon I will have to leave for England, because I have to do something for myself, for when I am older," explained Frances quietly.

"Mummy thinks you are too old for us now and we have to get somebody of sixteen or seventeen again."

"I understand that, Deirdre," said Frances. "I will miss you both."

"I won't really miss you!" said Deirdre, "but Ronan might". Frances knew the child was right.

In two days the holidays would be over and Frances made attempts at packing most of the children's clothes and went to bed.

Next morning Mrs Woods was in a gloomy mood. "You caused us great inconvenience last evening," she said to Frances. "I think you are old enough now to look for another job and I'll look for another junior."

The packing kept Frances very busy and her mind went over the eighteen months she spent with the family. she had grown up a little more. She had experienced family life at its best. She was confident in caring for children. She knew that the Woods, especially Ronan would be very special in her memory. When they arrived home to Clontarf Frances spent a few days washing and ironing the children's clothes and her own clothes, and generally settled the children back into normal routine. Mrs Woods paid her 10/6 for the month. Frances had her bag packed and didn't make any special effort to say goodbye to the children. She hated to say goodbye and as soon as she could she slipped away and walked to Clontarf Road and took the bus to Dublin City.

Identification cards for England had to be collected as well as the ticket to Holyhead. With everything ready Frances took a bus to say goodbye to Mary and Sean and Eileen. They had tea together. Mary gave Frances a watch with a second hand, and black stockings. They had been very kind over many months. Frances wanted to leave early to call into Cleary's to see how much a navy-blue mac would be. If she couldn't afford one she would do without one, she thought, until she got paid in England - £7 a month, according to the information sheet.

Mary accompanied her to Dublin to see her off. The navy-blue macs were £2-17s-6d. Frances had enough money, and agreed to buy one. Mary took it to be wrapped, and she paid for it.

"Just a little parting gift," she told Frances. Frances was astounded. Her husband probably didn't earn much more.

"Mary, one day I will repay you that money," said Frances. When they arrived at the North Wall, Sean was already there waiting for them.

"Good luck, Frances, study well, and mind your religion and mind your company." Frances could only look at them. There were no words good enough for the gratitude she owed them. She mounted the gangway and Mary and Sean went out of sight.

Once again she was alone. She looked at her new watch and remembered Sean and Mary and Eileen. People were pouring on to the boat. Little Ronan would be in bed by now she thought. She moved into the second class lounge and withdrew the letter handed to her by the lady interviewer, "please proceed to the Deputy Matron's Office on arrival." She wished she had Tessie's address. There was no hope now of ever finding her. She thought of writing to Mrs Woods, but that might upset the children. She wondered about Bunny, and Mary Crumlin and Rosanna, they must be out of the school now. They were all similar ages.

The anchors were raised, the ship was moving. The lights of Dun Laoghaire were growing more distant. The music played in the lounge:

"I saw those harbour lights
They only told me we were parting."

Then she realised that, sadly, she was leaving her own country. Whatever life had in store, success, failure, love, marriage, children, she started from here, and Ireland would always be special to her. Mother Brendan's poem came into her mind:

"Where'er are scattered the Irish nation
In foreign lands or on Irish ground
In every calling or rank or station
Good men and true men will always be
found."

The nuns at Sunday's Well would move with her, in her mind, all her life. They had cared for her, educated her, and denied themselves the pleasures of life so that underprivileged children would benefit from their total sacrifice and dedication. One day she might even see sense in Mother Thérèse's method.

CHAPTER FIFTEEN

The sea was rough. She felt seasick. She walked out on deck. The ship's nurse saw her leaning against the railing.

"Don't look at the water, better still come with me," said the nurse. She led Frances down to the cabin.

"Lie down in there, and I'll call you in the morning. No-one will disturb you there," she added. Frances was so grateful. She fell asleep to the sound of the engine.

The jingling of cups woke her. Frances looked up, "We are just coming in to Holyhead," said the nurse "have this cup of tea. I hear you are going to do your nurse training," said the nurse, with a smile.

"How did you know?" said Frances.

"A policeman came aboard before we sailed and asked me to look after you. Said you were from a Convent School and not used to travel," said the nurse.

"Humm, that was my friend. Sean," replied Frances. "Are you Irish?" Frances asked.

"Heavens, you don't know much about accents, then," said the nurse, "No, I'm from Holyhead see, you'll soon meet plenty of Welsh girls, and don't ask them if they are Irish. They might ask you if you were Scottish!" she laughed. The joke went over Frances's head.

"Don't matter, you'll soon pick up the jokes. Most Irish girls get too cute with nurse training. Have a nice wash and tidy up and take care of yourself. You'll enjoy your training. I loved my student days.

Great fun we had. Anyway, why are you training in England, Wales is nicer! See!"

The nurse left. Frances looked in the mirror. Her face was ghastly white. She picked up her travel bag and stepped outside. the nurse was busy in a room as Frances went by, she stopped to thank the nurse.

"A pleasure, don't mention it. You're not a good traveller. Still, with the money student nurses earn you won't be travelling much! Mind the step there, and take that train there to London."

The train to Euston was packed. Frances found a corner and stood by an open window. The guard's accent was very difficult to understand. She caught a word here and there. It was a melodic tone that seemed to lose the end of the words. At Crewe Station the train stopped and many alighted. Frances saw a vacant seat. She moved her travel bag near to her. In the past eighteen months she had acquired a few nice items. A nice dressing gown. She knitted herself some jumpers, bought nice underwear and nighties. Mrs Woods had given her lots of pieces of make-up over the months. Her shoes were neat and light. She had slippers and the navy-blue mac Mary had bought. Her watch she would treasure. She smiled to herself as she remembered the heavy brogues that Mother Thérèse gave her. They were so awful. She closed her eyes and imagined Sunday's Well. The picture was so clear in her mind. The lovely yellow distempered steps up through the centre of the lawn, with the large flower pots on either side. The shrubs in bloom, the grass neatly cut, and Saturdays when the children ran about with rakes and hoes and shovels. Mother Stanislaus's face of amazement at seeing Frances sitting in the back of General Costello's car! One day, maybe, she would get a chance to visit. It had not been a bad place to grow up in. Leaving there, she lacked confidence and she needed to be able to judge character to protect herself. Streetwise, now that would have been a bonus for someone alone! Well, whatever was to come, Frances was willing to face the challenge. She looked about her. A guard entered her carriage.

"Tickets, please!" Frances opened her handbag and withdrew her ticket. "Dublin to Euston" it read. The man clipped the corner of her ticket and in handing it back to her he held on to her hand. Frances looked up at him. He smiled at her. She felt embarrassed, but she smiled a thank you. He let go her hand. The young woman opposite her slid the door across after him. She looked at Frances.

"You should have said, 'Let go my hand or I'll slap your face, see." Frances smiled, she liked the young woman's accent.

"Did he do wrong?" asked Frances.

"God, Almighty," said Frances's companion, laying stress on the "ty", "he was after you, that's what he was, you'd better take care of yourself. Have you been here before?" she asked.

"No, this is my first time in England, I'm going to be a student nurse," answered Frances.

"Sure to goodness, you've a lot to learn. You're in Wales now, for another half hour anyway. My name is Nora, officially, but our Mam calls me Nesta." "Are you going to Euston," said the young woman.

"Yes, to Euston, and my name, well, officially it's Margaret, but everyone calls me Frances."

183

"Did your Mam not like Margaret?" asked Nesta, with a smile.

"I don't know, I grew up in a Convent School. I thought my name was Frances but when I left and looked at my Birth Certificate it shows as Margaret. My mother and father's names are correct, so it must be mine," said Frances with a frown.

"No worry then, you'll have to call yourself Margaret for all official use, so starting new at the hospital you might as well forget Frances, easy, see," said Nesta.

"In all official matters I'm Nora, see, only to our Mam I'm Nesta. You have to follow your Birth Certificate," Nesta added. "My mother is dead," said Frances. It was the first time in her entire life that she had said those words, and it came out so easy.

"Terrible to have no Mam," said Nesta. "People can be bastards, but you're Mam will always listen," said Nesta. "Did she die recently or in the war," asked Nesta.

"No, when I was six years old. I wasn't sure for years. No-one told me for sure for some time. Then one day a nun told me in her anger. But thank you for your help with my name. I'll use Margaret, new name and new life," laughed Frances.

"Nesta, you made a remark that I don't understand, you said people were bastards," said Frances.

"Oh, goodness, I'm sorry. It's not a good word, swearing it is, don't use it, I'm sorry!"

"Oh, Nesta, thank you very much. I've been trying to swear to fit in, you know. I don't know any words. Could you tell me a few more?" asked Frances.

"No! Oh, God, our Mam will die laughing when I tell her. I never used to swear, but when the bombs were dropping our Grandad used to say "Bastard Germans" so much that I picked it up. You don't want to swear. I'm at a Teacher Training Course in London, see, and when you hear the kind of language that I hear you won't want to repeat it," said Nesta, as she shook her head to emphasise her horror. "In nursing you might not hear so much. You'll fit in alright, you don't need to swear."

Frances noticed the demolished buildings and sites. She mentioned them to Nesta.

"The war, see," said Nesta. "'Twas the war. Thousands were killed."

"We heard something about a war, but not much," said Frances, hoping for more detail.

"Heard of it, is that all?" Nesta raised her eyebrows in surprise.

"That's all," said Frances hungry for news.

"Well, 'twas terrible. Our Mam had a nervous breakdown. Our Dad was taken prisoner, see, in Japan. He was rescued after the Japs surrendered, skin and bones he was. You want to hear him tell stories of the Jap camps, awful, awful, I tell you," said Nesta.

"Ireland was safe," said Frances, "I wonder why," she added.

"Wouldn't help us, would they," said Nesta. "Churchill asked if we could use their ports to repair our ships, but the Irish said no, so they got off, see, pleased the Jerry it did."

"Did we really refuse to help?" asked Frances in shame.

"'Tis a fact, see, no matter, we don't hold a grudge, "'tisn't your fault, my love," Nesta laughed. "See those buildings broken and cracked that's all war damage too. It was terrible, so many died, children, men, women, nurses, doctors, even ambulances were blown to bits. For five years every day and every night," said Nesta. Frances felt sad and uninformed in general.

"The nuns didn't tell us about the war," Frances said quietly.

"Hey, cheer up," said Nests, "it's over now, see, and you were just a kid. There'll always be wars. Men, you see, they have to war."

"My father was in the British Army," said Frances, "in France."

"See, he helped. Here have a sandwich," said Nesta. They chatted on and covered many subjects. Nesta was so easy to talk to. Frances loved the way she kept saying "see" at the end of sentences.

Nesta had been home to Wales to visit her mother at the weekend. They were nearing London. Built-up areas, churches, schools. Construction work was going on everywhere. Nesta pointed out prefabricated buildings.

"Thousands were homeless," explained Nesta, "so these are temporary homes. They can erect them very quickly. They don't look good, but they are only emergency homes," explained Nesta. "I wish you success in your nursing. You'll be OK, there are lots of Irish nurses," encouraged Nesta. "This is Euston, now."

Frances gathered up her bag in readiness to alight. Euston Station was enormous to Frances. The hustle and bustle, people carrying luggage. Soldiers, sailors in groups carrying sacks and bags. American Air Force men in groups or with girls. Lady porters! Ladies smoking! This was London.

Nesta helped her to the tube line to reach her hospital. They said goodbye, they had exchanged addresses on the train. Frances was fascinated by the tube train. So fast. The automatic doors! She expected someone entering to be squashed to bits! Ingenious. How Bunny and Mary Crumlin would love this invention, thought Frances. She got out fast as the door opened, in case of ill luck on her first day in her father's country. She made her way with the other passengers towards the exit. Up the moving staircase, she was so excited she wanted to get to the top of the escalator and shout out, "hey everybody this is so wonderful! I have never in my wildest moments imagined anything like it." But she remembered to remain dignified and seek help from the newspaper seller if she was unsure which way to turn for the hospital. That was Nesta's advice. She did just that and listened carefully to his instructions. She was thankful that he used his hand to point in the direction, she hardly understood one word.

"Dan air" must have meant, "down there"! she thought. Carrying her bag and stressed from travelling since the previous evening, she took comfort in the fact that she was almost at her destination. She turned left and could see the hospital building. The porter at the main gate took her name, and instructed her to keep left and follow the sign for the Deputy Matron. It was easy enough and Frances knocked on the door.

"Come in," said a lady's voice. Frances entered. The lady was in uniform. A dark navy dress and white frilly cap.

"Your name, please"

"Fran, em, Margaret Donnelly. I travelled from Dublin."

"Oh yes, do sit down. I am the Deputy Matron. I won't keep you a moment, you must be so tired. There are twelve of you to arrive. Three Irish and nine English. Your two countrywomen arrived earlier this morning, they are from Limerick, Lynch and O'Brien. You may rest tomorrow, and get yourself in order, but all twelve of you must be here, outside this office the following morning, to be taken for uniform fitting. I'll get someone to help you to the Nurses Home now." She left her office for a moment and returned with a young man.

"Here you are, help this student nurse to Mrs Rawlinson at the Nurses Home. Off you go, and may I say you are very welcome," said the Deputy Head with a nice smile. Frances followed her helper down a long corridor and left on to a courtyard and over to the Nurses Home. they walked in silence mostly, apart from the young man saying he wasn't a porter and that he was fed up being treated like one. At the door of the Nurses Home Frances thanked the young man who seemed rather sorry he had grumbled and he apologised. Mrs Rawlinson opened the door and immediately Frances liked her.

"Come in, my pet, you must be dead tired," she said to Frances.

"I am a little tired now," said Frances. "I think the rough sea didn't help," she added.

"I'll take you to your room." Mrs Rawlinson took her to the first floor, Room 28. Deadly quiet. Mrs Rawlinson spoke almost in a whisper. "Your Irish colleagues are sleeping. They arrived this morning. You'll meet them tonight, or in the morning. Put your clothes away. Have a nice bath, the bathrooms are just there," she pointed to a door opposite. "Then come down in your dressing gown and slippers and I'll make you a cup of tea before you sleep. By the way, I'm the warden of the Nurses Home."

"Thank you," said Frances, "may I miss the tea, please, as I am so very tired," she asked.

"Certainly, I understand, and now here is your key, keep it with you always," and with those words she tiptoed down the stairs. Frances had a very bright and pleasant room. She took her clean clothes to the bathroom and ran the bath. The bath refreshed and relaxed her. She moved her travel bag tidily into a corner and got into bed. It was 3 p.m. She had hardly put her head on the pillow when there was a gentle knock on her door. She got out of bed and opened the door.

"Hello, are you from Ireland?"

"Yes," said Frances, standing in her nightie and bare feet.

"Can we come in for a minute, we can't talk in the corridor because the night nurses are asleep."

"Yes," said Frances confused and tired.

"I'm Helen, this is Noreen, we heard you were coming. We arrived in England yesterday. We stayed last night in Hammersmith with my sister," said Helen and we arrived here this morning. The warden thinks we are tired!" said Noreen. Frances smiled and said that she was very pleased to meet them, but she was very tired.

"OK," said Helen, "go to bed, we'll call you about 7 and we can all go to 7.30 p.m. breakfast together," said Helen. "7.30 p.m. breakfast is for the night staff and we can go if we wish according to Mrs Rawlinson," advised Noreen.

"Four hours sleep, I will not be able to eat, I'll be so tired," said Frances. "We could meet tomorrow morning as soon as you like," suggested Frances.

"We'll knock at 7 and see how you are," said Helen.

"OK," said Frances.

"By the way, what is your name?" asked Noreen.

"Margaret, Margaret Donnelly."

"OK Margaret, we'll knock at 7." Frances climbed back into bed. What a day it had been. She was now across the sea in another country. What did life have in store. She was soon asleep.

If Noreen and Helen had knocked, Frances did not wake up because when she eventually woke up it was 6 a.m. the next morning. She felt so much better. She got up, and unpacked her bag into the chest of drawers by the window. Her room overlooked the tennis courts. She stripped her bed to air it, and took her key and clean clothes to the bathroom. By the time she was dressed and her bed made up, another hour had gone by. She was unsure what to do about breakfast, but she wasn't hungry. She decided to write to Mary and Sean and was settling down to the task when Noreen and Helen arrived. Frances had her door wide open. Frances greeted them and apologised for oversleeping.

"We didn't knock, we decided you looked very tired," said Noreen.

"Come to breakfast and we can talk," they invited. "Take your key with you, if you lose it, it is reported, you'll have to pay for a new one to be cut," said Noreen. They passed the warden's office and she asked if they had slept well. They assured her they were all very well and were going over to breakfast.

"Ah," said Mrs Rawlinson, "take these empty jars, they are clean. When you get to the dining room, the maid will fill them with your sugar ration as you are new. Sugar and sweets are still on ration here you know," said the warden. The girls took the jars and thanked her. They had no idea what sugar ration was all about until they arrived at the dining room. They crossed the tennis courts and cut through "Outpatients" and into the nurses dining room.

It was bedlam. So many nurses, a maid approached them. She took their names. They were expected. She was pleased to see that they had jars with lids! She filled each jar with sugar. She put a strip of sticking plaster across the jar and wrote their name on each. That sugar had to last them one month. It was up to each of them to economise. Noreen said she'd write to her mother for sugar and share it! Frances told them that she had no-one to ask for sugar so she would "go easy" on the sugar ration. They had cornflakes, eggs, bacon and tea and toast. Frances had no bacon. Within a very short time they were joined by some more new students and a surprise for Noreen, Helen and Frances, they were joined by another Irish girl, Maura Holt from St. Mary's of the Isle, Cork City and one young man

191

from Mauritius. Frances was delighted. Maura was delightful. eventually they numbered thirteen students. Eight English girls and four Irish, and one Mauritian. The day was their own and the Irish girls felt comfortable together. Helen and Noreen were school friends. Their parents were neighbours in Limerick, Ireland.

Frances explained her circumstances, though not in detail, just that her mother died when she was very young, and that the nuns had brought her up. Frances believed Maura had a story, but Maura kept her business to herself. Noreen and Helen were exceptionally kind to Frances. They accepted the name "Margaret" for official use.

Next morning the whole group gathered around the Deputy Matron's office and were taken to the uniform room. The supervisor in the sewing room was efficient if formidable, a large lady. Each student was given three dresses, fourteen aprons, six caps, a light blue belt and a navy cape lined in red. They watched as the supervisor demonstrated folding a cap. Each nurse had to fold one cap to satisfy the supervisor. Uniform was signed for. The students were made well aware that it remained the property of the hospital, and any lost item would be at the nurse's expense. The supervisor then wished them all a successful training. She invited them to call on her reference any uniform problem. The group returned to the Nurses Home to deposit their heavy load and to dress in uniform to meet the Hospital Registrar for a medical, to be carried out in the Nurses Sick Bay. The medicals took two hours to complete the examining of all of the thirteen students. Then Mrs

Rawlinson shepherded them back to the Nurses Common Room to meet Matron. She was waiting for them. That was their first meeting with their Matron. They soon realised they had little to worry about. Miss Morris was a huge lady. She was blessed with a beautiful face and within a few minutes listening to her, the girls felt certain that they had an excellent leader.

"Welcome, everyone," she began. "Your training commences tomorrow at 9 a.m. Your tutors are Miss White and Mr Luxton. Anatomy and Physiology will be Miss White's responsibility and all other subjects will be shared by both tutors. I hope you all have navy gabardines. You will wear them on trips to dairies, sewage works and waterworks. Watch the noticeboards. Knowing where you should be and when is your responsibility. Your progress will be assessed weekly and your behaviour observed. There will be an opportunity on one day a week, after the first six weeks, for each of you to spend one day on the wards. After twelve weeks an examination will confirm your progress. Anyone who fails will be asked to leave. Training each one of you is extremely expensive." Matron stared at the new intake during her pause.

"Late nights require late passes. We cannot have tired nurses. The patients would not benefit. In three and a half year's time, those of you who reach the State final Examination will also have their behaviour file observed by the Examiner. Your record of behaviour is as important as any academic ability. The Examiner reads each file carefully." She dropped her voice to emphasise her meaning. She stood up and smiled. She wished the group a happy and successful training. She left the group to Mrs Rawlinson who advised them to check that they had pencils, coloured pencils, erasers, and a ruler. They broke up into friendly twos or threes to go to the town, to W.H. Smiths to make the purchases advised.

They walked the mile to the main shopping centre. Anything from radios to radiograms and refrigerators were on sale on Hire Purchase. That system was not in Ireland at that time. There were many clothes shops, and one in particular, on a corner position. It had a bride's dress in the window. It was the most beautiful dress Frances had ever seen. She had never seen a wedding, let alone been a guest at one. The other girls were anxious to buy their necessities. Frances was spellbound at the sight of the fairytale dress in the window. The delay by the girls at the window brought the owner out to investigate. He was a chubby little man of about sixty years.

"And vot can ve do for you young ladies?" he asked. They all just giggled and made to walk off.

"Vait a moment," he said, "I haf the beautiful coats for you inside, come, come," he urged. Frances and her colleagues felt trapped and although they didn't go inside they stopped by the shop door.

"Vere are you young ladies goink?" the old gentleman asked.

"We are commencing our nurse training and we need some pencils and paper, and we are on our way to the stationery shop," volunteered Noreen.

"Vell, if you nurses vant coats for the vinter, come to me soon, £1 every month and in September you vill haf a beautiful coat," he said, clasping his hands over and over again.

"Thank you sir, we will," said Noreen just to get away. Frances couldn't forget the magnificent white dress. On their way back to the hospital they met Mrs Rawlinson. She greeted them, and mentioned that she was on her way to the post office. She told them that the Catholic Priest was at the Nurses Home taking tea with the other nurses and that he would be pleased to meet them.

"You'll all have to join the 'Catholic Nurses Guild'" she said. "The Priest will tell you all about it and Doctor Hefferman is another contact in that Guild," she added. "See you all later," she said and left the girls to continue their way back to the hospital, and she went off to the post office.

The Priest was delighted to meet them. He gave each nurse some paperwork bearing information about the "Guild". Meetings once a month at the local convent. He stressed that in their training no Catholic nurse should ever assist at a termination of pregnancy. Frances had no idea what the Priest meant. So much was said after that statement, on various subjects, that by the time the Priest left them no-one brought up anything for discussion. He was a young Priest, and became a familiar sight around the hospital. Even the non-Catholic nurses pulled his leg in the hallway.

"Afternoon Father," said one nurse.

"Are you one of us?" asked the smiling Priest.

"Not likely, Father, you lot are far too strict for me," the nurse replied, laughingly.

The girls returned to their rooms on the first floor, they agreed to meet in Noreen's room by 7 p.m. and go to dinner together. Frances checked over her stationery, and placed everything necessary neatly in a pencil case. She enjoyed a hot bath and relaxed in her dressing gown by her room window overlooking the tennis courts, and wrote her first letter to Mother Thérèse. She found the task very difficult.

While writing she could visualise the nun's face and then heard the voice of the mistress saying "the devil lives inside you". No, it was impossible. She tore up the half written letter. She wondered if she could write to Mother Philomena. Maybe it would cause trouble, and yet, how nice it would be, to tell Mother Philomena all her news and to ask if Rosanna was in Australia or America! Bunny? what had happened to her, did she become a nun?

There was a strong bond between Frances and the Convent. Through all the months caring for Deirdre and Ronan in Dublin, she remembered and applied method and organisation, cleanliness, fair play and a commitment to duty. She knew that the Convent was so far away and, yet, it was as if she was always within its shadow. The springtime, she visualised the daffodils and the crocuses. Summertime, the shrubbery in bloom and Mother Stanislaus busy overseeing the work in progress, on Saturdays, as the children helped to cut the lawns and weed the walks. Frances lived from day to day. She found difficulty in planning ahead. Her colleagues made suggestions reference recreation, and it was easy to follow their ideas. For so many years Frances worked to order, to the sound or signal of a bell. With Mrs Woods, Frances followed instructions. Now she was alone. It was frightening, but she would not discuss the

196

problem. She would observe others, and take one day at a time. Buying the pencils at the shop in town was successful only because she followed Helen's and Noreen's choice. She wrote a letter to Sean, Mary and Eileen. She thanked them sincerely for all the kindness they had shown to her, and gave them as much news as she could remember.

She also wrote to Nesta. She lay down on her bed and allowed her mind to drift back to the nurse on board the British ferry. Further back to the Woods, to the two small children that she missed, and wondered if they would ever again meet. Then to the sea wall, that early cold morning when the Gárda happened along. How fortunate she was that he was kind enough to help her. And his sweet wife who helped her to find peace of mind. Looking back, since the journey from Cork, Frances found little to congratulate herself on. The Costello job was tough, so she ran away. Kathleen and Tessie took no time in winning her over to take the job with Mrs Woods. Basically it was Mary Tierney who encouraged her to train as a nurse.

The inability to make decisions was a weakness Frances would have to control. She knew it could not be an easy future. People were difficult for Frances to handle. Those who smiled a lot were not always on her side. She discovered that fact in Mrs Woods. It seemed to Frances that there were those who achieved by maintaining two faces, and those who suffered from them, either because of their naïveness, although they were usually decent people. The very bright who were capable of calculating in seconds the advantages or disadvantages. The ditherers who were swallowed up by every kind. Frances was a ditherer. She realised the fact and accepted the challenge to change.

How difficult the battle would be, it was not easy to assess. She wanted to find a way to save herself from people. They were her greatest fear. Helen and Noreen seemed genuinely friendly. A couple of the English girls had complimented Frances's knitting when she wore her hand-made sweater. Frances immediately offered to knit for them and they responded by offering to sew for her and to do her hair when necessary.

There was a sewing machine in the Nurses Home for the use of any nurse. A grand piano donated by a grateful patient according to the plaque attached. The one male student from Mauritius seemed to feel more comfortable with the English girls. The Irish girls had never met black people. The only knowledge they had concerning black people was from reading the Catholic Missionary magazines. The Irish had a preconceived idea that all black people were either savages or Catholic converts! That their conversion to Catholicism and therefore civilisation was due to the work of priests and nuns! These missionaries who walked about in heat, flies and among lepers and witch doctors to find lost souls. Every Catholic magazine called for "Pennies for Black babies". there in their midst sat an educated and refined young black man. The Irish girls felt shy and a little superior. Batu was his name.

CHAPTER SIXTEEN

The Preliminary Training School opened at 9 a.m. Thirteen students was the full complement. Miss White was not far off retirement age and Mr Luxton was nearly fifty years old. There were two lecture rooms. One room was used for theoretical study and the second for practical work. The tutors worked tirelessly to help the students. Miss White set them test papers every week to assess progress. Frances enjoyed the course and learned more than she had ever bargained for.

When eventually they reached the Reproductive Tract, male and female organs were discussed in detail. Frances was seated next to Batu. For the first time she learned the "facts of life". The embarrassment she felt was lessened a little by the fact that all heads were bent over note books. What, she thought, was Miss White talking about? What happened to the babies under the gooseberry bushes? The vans diferens, the scrotal sac, the penis and their functions, the vagina, the cervix, fallopian tubes and finally how the sperm got there. She could feel her cheeks burning with embarrassment, and then, shock. She loved children, but surely no decent Catholic girls would do that! It must be the English, she thought. The Protestants must have devised that method! There had to be an alternative if she was to have any children! Miss White went on and on and drew diagrams on the blackboard. How could Frances lift her head and look at the blackboard! And Batu sitting next to her. Frances wondered if he had "one".

She wondered if priests didn't have one, then she realised they had to have one to urinate. Oh, it was all such a worry. Would that lecture ever end? Frances gave up listening and waited for the lunch bell. Miss White cleaned the blackboard and dismissed the class. Lynch leaned over to Frances and whispered,

"I thought women coughed up babies!" The English girls took it all in their stride. None of them had the slightest idea of the shock that lecture had been to some of their colleagues. Helen and Noreen, Frances and Maura had much to discuss and they agreed to meet in Noreen's room that night.

The first six weeks soon passed and the students were allocated to the wards on one day each week. Frances found the practical work interesting and very rewarding. She felt useful and helpful and it was good for her self esteem. It as an introduction to English people in general. The various dialects were curious and the patients were warm and friendly. Frances was allocated to Sister Rogers on Women's Surgical. Discipline was very strict, but a sense of humour, especially among the patients, made the Nurses' duties easier. By the penultimate week of the 12 weeks, Frances had sampled Female Surgical, Male Surgical, Orthopaedic, Male and Female and Children's Ward. The final week was spent revising, and eventually the PTS Exam. Only one girl failed. The group received new caps, and were allocated full time ward duties. All went on night duty. Frances was on Male Orthopaedics. Fractures, and many from road accidents kept Ward 8 very busy indeed.

Most patients were bed cases and heavy lifting left the Nurses quite tired at the end of the night. Patients from road accidents who died in Casualty were sent up to Ward 8 for "Last Office". Frances met her first sad case in that very early stage of training. Her Senior Nurse was an excellent help. He was a third year student who well remembered his first year. Frances was full of zeal and energy. She was upset and saddened by the untimely death of a young man who had been run over by a lorry, as he cycled home from town. She carried out her duties in Last Office and finally combed the thick fair hair that framed that young man's face. She attended the friends of the deceased in an understanding and sympathetic manner.

The young man who died was due to be married the following Saturday. He had arrived from Yugoslavia, to marry an English girl. The older gentleman, who gave Frances that information, was King Peter of Yugoslavia, in exile, as he stood with her in the Ward Office, on that sad night. Many nights were extremely busy. Surgical days meant very busy nights. There was always some lighthearted moments for patients and Nurses, and Frances enjoyed to see the patients happy. Helen and Noreen, Frances and Maura were often disappointed that their off-duty nights didn't coincide. Many mornings after a very busy night-duty the new first year group had to attend a lecture from 8.30 to 9.30 a.m. After the lecture they met to compare notes and enjoy a cup of coffee in Noreen's room. Often the time was as late as 12 noon before they went to bed. Such gatherings compensated for the loss of off-duty

together. On the rare occasion that any two did have
their off-duty time in harmony, with a friend the girls
usually set off for an evening at the "Garryowen" in
Hammersmith. Many Irish nurses enjoyed the great
Céile Bands that visited the Garryowen. They sought
late passes and that gave them the freedom to dance
until 10.30 p.m. Frances had never learned to dance.
Noreen and Helen were experts from their village
halls in Limerick.

"When we get our nights off together, we'll teach
you," promised Noreen. The Orthopaedic Ward was
well known as a "fun ward". Patients confined to bed
with healing fractures were otherwise quite healthy
and often bored. Early days after surgery were
indeed painful days for the patient. Pain killing
injections or oral help with similar medication was
administered according to the surgeon's written
instruction. When the effect of the drug wore off the
patients showed great heroism. If at times Mr
Bowden in bed six did call out in pain, Frances
rushed over to talk to him and to reassure him that it
was almost time for his next dose.

"Can I get you anything Mr Bowden," she asked
earnestly.

"Well, please Nurse, could you leave the pressure
points, the drugs round, the telephones and nip down
to our Fish and Chippie and get me Cod and Chips,
plenty of salt," Mr Bowden teased, and winked his
fatherly eye. It was so easy to "pull her leg". Frances
had much to learn about the British sense of humour.
The nursing colleagues on the Ward were aware of
Nurse Donnelly's "green streak" and great fun was
had at her expense.

One night about 11 p.m., and just before Night Sister's round, some off-duty Nurses were returning from the town dances Helen entered the ward through the French doors at the far end. She had heard so much from Frances about brave Mr Bowden that she brought him fish and chips! Before Helen had a chance to hand over his contraband, Night Sister appeared in the walkway to the ward. There was no time for Helen to leave.

"Quickly, into that bed," urged Frances. Fully clothed, shoes plus fish and chips went under the bed clothes. Mr Bowden's chips were so near, but so far! Sister greeted Frances,

"Good evening, nurse. Any new admissions?" And how many spare beds?" said Sister glancing down at the Day Report.

"No admissions and only one spare bed," said Frances, her heart was pounding. Even at the ward entrance she could smell the fish and chips! Dear God, thought Frances, I'll be thrown out, it's back to Mother Thérèse for me! She walked with Night Sister.

"This is Mr Jones, fractured femur."

Sister shone her torch in Mr Jones's face and woke him! Oh, God, Frances thought, Sister is in one of her enthusiastic moods! On to the next bed,

"Mr Carruthers, concussion." Frances was sure that Sister would hear her thumping heart. As the sister and nurse moved along Mr Bowden acted in time, just two beds from Helen, he yelled out,

"Nurse, nurse, please!"

"Shush," said Sister as she rushed to him, "you'll wake the other patients!"

"What about me then, I was asleep, free at last from pain, your torch shone here and woke me, and now the pain is back again," said Mr Bowden in a mood of distress. He fixed his eyes on Sister.

"Get me something for this pain, please Sister."

"Alright, let's see his notes, Nurse," and turned to walk to the ward office. Frances glanced down at her hero, and his devilish wink said a thousand words. Sister returned with Frances who had quickly prepared hot milk and two Codeine!

"I'll just take the milk, Nurse, the pain is easing off! Keep the tablet for some other poor sod!" said Mr. Bowden. The spare bed was empty and tidy! Sister cut short her round. Frances escorted her Nurse Officer to the ward door and thanked her.

"Keep an eye on Mr Bowden, Nurse, I think he had a nightmare. Wouldn't mind guessing that his visitors brought him fish and chips at 7.30! The ward reeks of the stuff, open some windows for a while!" said the Night Sister.

"I will, Sister," said Frances who couldn't wait to rush down the ward to thank dear Mr Bowden.

"That's alright love, your mate left me the chips, she lay on the fish! You'd better change that bed," said the patient. Dear Mr Bowden! Frances would miss him on his discharge.

The Senior Nurse arrived back from dinner. She had the first sitting 11 p.m. to 12 a.m. Frances reported "all well, except Mr Bowden, he's a little uncomfortable, nothing serious," said Frances, and she left to join Noreen and very likely, Helen, in the dining room. Helen, would hardly go to the Nurses' Home without hearing the end of the Fish and Chips episode!

Night duty ended. A great deal of experience had helped Frances to adjust to life in some ways. The British sense of humour was a tonic that she needed lots of. The group had two nights off, before going on to day duty. Female Surgical, Ward 7. Frances read on the change list. Sister Williams had a good reputation. Frances felt she would enjoy that Ward. Plenty of trays and trolleys to lay! Mastectomies were common, colostomies, hernia repairs, amputations. Solutions to dilute, washout to do, history taking, diagnosis sought and prognosis noted.

Every day at some pre-arranged time, early mornings or evenings lectures were well attended. Text books littered her room. Revision was constant. The female patients were very special to Frances. Very soon she saw how important the Mother was to a family. How otherwise wayward teenagers or older children would rally to Mum, and sit and worry and hope for her recovery. She saw the sacrifice Mums paid for their families. Most terminal cases had sought no early help for the same reason - "could not leave the children".

Women tolerated pain far longer than men could. But one thing they all had in common, whether on male or female wards, they had tremendous care for each other's suffering. Always ready to help to call Nurse, or if possible to get a bed pan. To feed an older patient. On the male wards all elderly patients were called "Pop" by his fellow patients and on female wards the elderly ladies were affectionately called "Gran". Frances met all social levels. Every circumstance was a lesson for life, to adjust, to accept change, to adapt, to learn to live with the vain, the humble, the knowalls, the unassuming, and the haughty, the obnoxious and the sensitive. She hid among them and got through each day. Each evening she found time to shut herself in her room and think back over the day and the problems she met and dealt with. There was no book of wisdom, no-one to talk to, with experience of life. Her only recourse was the Convent and the nuns. She wouldn't dream of writing for advice. She was out, on her own two feet. She sat and tried to imagine what Mother Colette would do with the problems or what would Mother Good Counsel do?

Salaries were paid monthly and it made little difference to Frances. There was always someone with a hard luck story and Frances gave away her £7-10s-0d. She washed her blouses, and hung them to dry, in the small laundry room, at the Nurses Home, and someone stole them. She lacked the confidence to complain. When she actually saw the Nurse wearing it, she could only stare at the blouse and wonder how could she ever retrieve it!

One Saturday evening the group of Irish girls agreed to go dancing. Noreen promised to teach Frances to waltz to the music, when they reached the "Garryowen". They were a happy team. The entrance fee was fairly expensive. Nurses unaccompanied by a boy friend chatted casually by the entrance and eventually a couple of lads arrived and joined the girls. The unspoken plot was, one in, all in. So the two young men bought four tickets for the girls, if every one promised to dance with them, during the evening. Once inside Frances found another world. The band was lively. Most people were dancing and others were either drinking at the bar or seated in the restaurant area. The atmosphere was electric. They met a couple of their English colleagues, and one of them introduced Peter to Frances.

"I really can't understand a word he is saying," said the student nurse in a smug tone.

"Where is he from," asked Frances in a whisper.

"No idea," said her colleague and off she went, leaving Frances to talk to Peter.

"Where are you from?" asked Frances slowly and clearly.

"From Poland," he answered defensively. Frances felt a sudden pain of nostalgia.

"Poland," she repeated, her eyes were full of surprise.

"Do you know Poland?" Peter asked earnestly.

"Oh no," said Frances, "but I am so pleased to know you, because when I was at school I remember, in fact I'll never forget, that underneath my tin plate and little mug were the words 'made in Poland'" Frances's eyes filled with tears as she visualised the convent, the nuns, her school friends. She excused herself and walked to the Ladies Room. Returning to the dance floor she saw Peter waiting for her.

"I can't dance," she told her friend.

"I'll teach you," said Peter. They enjoyed a five minute dance lesson and moved on to the restaurant. Peter explained that although he loved dancing, he found that the girls were shy or afraid of foreigners.

"But I am a foreigner from Ireland," said Frances, "and so are my friends. How did you get here?" asked Frances.

"The war, and the army. I was in a German concentration camp, Dachau, for a time. I managed to get away and the Yugoslav Partisans found me, it is a long story," said Peter. "Eventually I joined the Polish Fifth Division and I was in a big battle at Monte Cassino in Italy. After the war I couldn't return to Poland because my part of Poland went to Stalin. I have lost all my family," he said. Frances observed him closely while he spoke. There was hurt in his eyes. At that time she had not the slightest idea of his experiences in his young life.

"And now," she encouraged more detail.

"I work, I play, I learn to live. It is difficult with no family, no feeling of belonging, no purpose worthwhile to aim for," he went on. Frances understood exactly. Her problems were similar.

"Well," said Frances, "you know me, and I am not afraid of a foreigner," she added.

"May I meet you again," he asked.

"Yes," said Frances, I am free again tomorrow. Come to the hospital tomorrow evening about 7 p.m."

They discussed life in general. He was grateful to England for the freedom he enjoyed. He aimed to marry, to own his own house. He loved children. Frances thought deeply if she could cope with such responsibility. Suddenly Peter said,

"Would you marry me?" It was an ordinary question to Frances, she was neither surprised nor flattered.

"You need a family to help you, Peter. I have no one. I grew up in a Convent School. I have no family, I am over here alone, and like you I am trying to fit into the jig-saw puzzle that life is," she explained.

"Then we are right for each other," he urged. "Together we will build our lives. We will have children, and no one will ever hurt them while we are alive," he paused. Frances was hearing Mother Thérèse, "You will go to the devil".

"Peter," said Frances with an impish eye, as he waited for her answer, "are you the Devil?"

"No, I don't think so!" said Peter with humble surprise and smiled. "Then I'll marry you," said Frances, "I don't know when, but I will."

"For now," he said with a hug, "we will be best friends, we are no longer alone in the world." The music stopped for a moment or two. The relief was appreciated by couples or groups involved in conversation, who were otherwise nearly hoarse trying to be heard! Noreen came bounding to Frances and Peter.

"Come on, this is the Walls of Limerick, anyone can follow their leader, come on, you'll enjoy it," she pleaded. It was a fun dance and so popular that there was an encore! It demanded plenty of energy and it preceded the last waltz. It didn't take too long for Frances to get the hang of it. Peter was a strong leader. The M.C. announced the date of the band's next assignment at the Garryowen. He thanked everyone for attending and urged them to travel home safely. The happy group had escorts on their way to the hospital. Peter chatted to Frances all the way. He had so many questions and only laughed at all the negative replies.

"Have you been to Kew Gardens?" he asked her.

"No," she replied.

"Seen Kensington Gardens?" he asked.

"No," she answered.

"What about Buckingham Palace, Trafalgar Square, Hyde Park?" he asked.

"No, no, no. I haven't been anywhere, I have no money," she added.

"Don't you get paid?" he queried.

"Oh, yes, but I gave it to a nurse who needed help going home to Ireland, she promised to give it back," said Frances, with not a care in the world.

"Well, I can assure you that you will not get it back," said Peter slowly and quietly, and his accent was clearly foreign, but not unpleasant to listen to. "It is very hard for me," said Frances, "I have no courage. I wanted to decline but the word 'no' would not come out," she went on.

"Take my advice," said Peter, "they will think that you are a fool, they won't see your good nature, they will take and take and you will end up with nothing. See if I am correct, wait until the end of the month," he said. Frances agreed to check his theory. They all walked together to the hospital gates and then said goodnight. Peter promised to call on her the following evening. Frances thanked him for a very happy evening. He gave her a peck on her cheek and walked away. That peck on the cheek was the first kiss that Frances could ever remember since 28th October 1939 when Granny kissed them goodbye.

"What's he like?" asked the gang of three.

"Very nice," said Frances "He is coming to visit tomorrow evening again," she added.

"Don't get serious with him, please," pleaded Noreen. "You've too much study, and anyway he is a foreigner," said Noreen.

"I don't mind if he is a foreigner. He is just a friend and in time I will know if he is a good type," said Frances.

"How are you going to know?" said Maura, "you think everyone is good. It's the convent you went to, the nuns think everyone is an angel," added Maura, with a certain bitterness in her voice.

"Well," said Frances, "let me tell you that my nuns were very well able to tell good from bad, and I will learn, even if I learn the hard way. Peter is polite, respectful, clean and tidy. I noticed his fingernails and his shoes. He gave me some good advice. He is my friend and I would like you to be nice to him when he calls, you will, won't you," asked Frances and she looked more to Helen and Noreen.

"Of course we will," said Helen, "he is very nice." They reached the Nurses Home and went quietly to their rooms.

The next day was spent mostly revising. Helen and Noreen joined Frances in her room for tea and toast. They took turns to entertain in their rooms. Tea and toast was usual. Other times it was chicken noodle soup and lemonade. The small kitchen downstairs was near Mrs Rawlinson's office and the key had to be got from her, and returned, by the nurse in question. Noreen and Helen often talked of their home and family. They wrote home once a week. Noreen missed one week, and her father wrote a letter and Noreen gave his letter to Frances to read. He was so upset and angry, that she had missed one letter, and caused great worry in the home. After that they never missed a weekly newsletter home.

Peter arrived on time and Frances left with him for a long walk. He arrived in England in 1947 with the Polish army and was billeted in Hampshire, in the small village of Odiham. Frances was interested in the war and why it started. There were nearly eleven years missing of the outside world in her life.

"Tell me your story, from the beginning," she asked Peter. They walked for nearly two hours. Peter talked, Frances was enthralled by his story. His part of Poland was invaded by the Germans and by the Russians. In 1941 he was arrested by the Gestapo and accused of belonging to the Polish Underground Movement. After a cruel interrogation he was thrown on to a train of wooden wagons. Hundreds of people, men, women and children were squashed into those wagons. There was no ventilation and all had their heads shaved and covered in a chemical that burned and pained their scalps. After what seemed like endless hours, they were released from the wagons near a camp. The camp was called Dachau.

Many nationalities were held there. On arrival many old people were dead in the wagons. Fear and terror was on the faces of the inmates who watched their arrival. Jews were there, simply for being Jewish. Other nationals were guilty of political charges, from young members of freedom fighters to those who were termed spies. There were German citizens too. Any German who rebelled against the Nazi system was deemed to be an enemy. Peter had been whipped by a German guard before his journey to Dachau. A German doctor, who was a prisoner, attended to his wounds that wer suppurating. There was no antibiotic treatment. The doctor merely kept the wounds as clean as he could, and encouraged Peter to eat anything, and everything that he was given. The doctor and Peter became good helpful members within the pitiful crowd of victims, that the evilness within the German government intended to murder. Peter, although just fourteen years old was set to work on an outside working party project, to make a passage through some rocky hills.

Older members planned an escape. On a given signal, one day, many months later Peter ran off with other prisoners. Guards had been killed, shots were fired that alerted other guards from the camp. He ran as fast as he could. The sound of barking dogs grew fainter. Peter fell into wet leaves and lay there. He was certain that the guards and dogs would find him. He didn't much care. He was ready to die. He felt sure his family were dead. He fell asleep. He remembered opening his eyes and seeing a big heavy-looking woman looking down at him. Her heavy black clothes reached her ankles. She pointed a rifle at him. Peter was calm and ready to die. The woman shouted at him. He couldn't understand the language. It wasn't German. He tried Polish. She understood a little. Peter realised that she wanted his name, and where he came from. He explained as best he could that he came from Dachau, that day.

"No," she said, "escape from Dachau was four days ago." She bent down and with a little effort she picked him up and threw him across her shoulder. With the aid of the rifle as a walking stick she walked with her bundle to a cave. When inside and deep into the cave, he saw hundreds of people in fairly good condition. Many were children. They rushed to help Peter. They were kind and generous to him. He was very weak. Over many days they fed himwell, and he learned that they were loyal supporters of the Yugoslav Royal Family. They fought under Mihailovich, and they enlisted Peter's help as soon as he felt strong enough. Over many months he fought with them. They were known as the Yugoslav Partisans (Chetniks) under Mihailovich. They disagreed with Tito and his communist ideas for the future.

One day Peter and a colleague were out on "business" when they came upon two soldiers. Not certain if the soldiers were American or British they made it known that they supported Churchill. Peter and his colleague were in rags and tatters. The soldiers disarmed them and gave them a drink from a black can. It was disgusting, but it was given with goodwill! The soldiers puzzled with the language, and decided to take the pair back to an officer. It was soon sorted out, that Peter and his mate were allies. "Take them to the Polish camp." The order was interpreted for Peter by the officer. That was how he met the Second Company of the Fifth Division of Polish Soldiers under British command. He travelled everywhere with Colonel Gnatowski, and on to the Battle of Monte Cassino.

After the war "Old Gnat" encouraged him to go to England, as part of Poland, where he was born, was no longer under a Polish Free Government. It was under the Soviet Communist rule. There was no religion and little freedom, and soldiers who had seen life in the West were murdered in thousands by Stalin on their return.

When the war ended Peter was nearly nineteen years old. He journeyed with the Army to England from Italy. By 1953 Peter had learned a great deal about life in England. He wrote to his mother on several occasions. No reply ever came. He was certain that his family was dead. He set his mind on settling in England. He hoped that one day his country would be free.

Frances was amazed at his courage and fighting spirit. He survived so much. She wondered if he hated Germans. She questioned him so.

"No I don't hate anyone. In every nationality there are good and bad people. The German Gestapo was evilness personified, but in due course their conscience would be their hell," he answered.

Peter had a great sense of humour. He had a most generous nature. Frances received a gift on every date! He was working as a trainee at a printers in Park Royal, North London. He was eager to improve his English, especially in spelling and writing. He had an excellent attitude to work but took life a bit too seriously. Maybe it was quite normal Frances thought, and simply in contrast to the Irish easy going nature of the young people she worked among, as forty percent were Irish.

"I want to learn about English culture and I want to speak good English before I apply for British naturalisation" he told her on several occasions.

"One day I want to own by business and my house, and then I will feel that I have some way achieved all that my family lost when the Germans invaded our village." His face was a mask of determination. Frances felt that the underlying force behind that ambition lay in his family pride in Lvov, Poland. Material achievement was one thing, but Frances was concerned that the love of his family and his homeland he so pined for would never leave him, until he returned, and left again, with a clear mind about their welfare. She was determined to help him to search for news.

One way or another her future with him could be harmed by their ghosts. He was, she felt, a good young man, but he had a broken heart, and maybe a broken mind. He found it difficult to erase the picture that was ever present in his mind of his mother on her knees before the Gestapo officer, pleading Peter's innocence.

She was kicked sideways to the ground by the German jackboot, as Peter was dragged away. Did she die? Was she just unconscious, and maybe survived? Would he ever find out? None of his letters were answered. Frances encouraged him to continue writing. She felt that in one way, at least, he was being helped by writing. In time healing would take place. Then again, maybe someone survived. A neighbouring farmer with knowledge of his family, perhaps. Frances wrote to the International Red Cross. They replied promptly and assured her that his family name and address was added to their 'Search List'. Their lists held hundreds of thousands of addresses. Frances found some evenings with Peter were indeed profoundly stressful as Peter discussed his war experiences in Dachau, and he worried about his mother and brother and sisters. If only there was some way she could help Peter. Eventually she had to advise him to put all worry of his family to one side, and to build his life in England. Maybe one day news would come West, and perhaps his mother, brother and sisters were all alive. Frances had her life to build, the way forward was tough enough, without the stress of Peter's experiences. They agreed to let each day unfold whatever was in store, and together they would cope.

Peter got on well at his work, and Frances continued her training. She was madly enthusiastic on duty, and always ready to report to ward sister as soon as each task was finished. She didn't waste a minute. Sister Williams would swing about and find Frances ready for the next assignment.

"For God's sake, Nurse, what do you want?"

"I've finished that colostomy washout", said Frances proudly.

"Well, go and help all those patients who have dentures. Collect them, and give each set a good clean, and don't forget visiting at 2.30 p.m.," said Sister, hoping the task would keep that over-zealous student nurse out of her way!

Frances went from bed to bed and collected dentures. No-one questioned the nurse.

"Come on, Mrs Sellen, let's have your teeth - I'm going to make them shine for you," said Frances. One or two patients seemed a little perplexed but were reassured by the student that all was well. Out in the sluice room in a sinkful of water, refreshed with glycothymolene, Frances had tumbled the fifteen to sixteen pairs of dentures. With a tiny but strong bristled brush she washed each set. Suddenly Sister Williams stood in the doorway.

"Nurse!" she yelled,

"Yes Sister," answered a puzzled nurse

"Who in the name of God owns those teeth?" and Sister put both her hands into the water to lift out as many as her hands could hold. Frances instantly saw the stupidity of her effort.

"Oh, Sister, I'm very sorry, I'll sort them out at once." Frances was panic-stricken. Sister Williams burst out laughing.

"You idiot girl, the visitors will be here soon. How are we going to know who owns what set?" Frances didn't laugh. She rinsed the load of dentures, some whole sets, others half sets with gaps, various pieces of two teeth on a bar, or three on a band of plastic.

One bowl of teeth, and one highly embarrassed nurse went from bed to bed asking

"Would you know your teeth!" Amazingly, the situation was resolved. The co-operation of the patients, only too ready to help nurse out of her predicament, saved her day! The patients and their relatives enjoyed the saga of the teeth in one bowl, for days!

Sister Williams was a good teacher who remembered her own student days and her mistakes. Ward 7 was a very busy ward, Tuesdays and Thursdays were surgical days and emergencies on other days added to the busy schedule. There were happy endings, mixed with sad reports. All handled with trained skill. In spite of very hectic days on duty the students had to attend lectures, and find time to study. Nights at the "Garryowen" in Hammersmith became fewer as study periods overtook recreation time.

One morning it fell to Frances, once again, to do Mrs Smith's colostomy washout. She enjoyed to reassure the patient, and to give her hope. To be discharged in the early fifties with a colostomy was quite traumatic for anyone. A little later Frances emptied all her instruments into the steriliser and stupidly included the gum elastic horn, never to be sterilised by boiling! It was eventually retrieved 25 minutes later, and had become the size of a thimble from the size of a small vase. Sister Williams went crazy! Not to mention the cost, there were only two in the hospital - one on the male surgical and one on the female surgical wards. A requisition was written by Sister, and Frances took it to Matron's office. The journey to the Admin section was, for Frances, a walk to the Gas Chamber!

She rehearsed and rehearsed her apology to Matron. I couldn't be more sorry? I'll pay for it? How the hell could she pay for it. Sister Williams said its cost was £90. Frances earned £7 a month! She met Helen on her journey.

"Where are you going?" enquired her friend, delighted for an opportunity to chat.

"I put the gum elastic horn into the steriliser and . . . ,

"What!" said Helen, in absolute astonishment, "don't you remember from PTS training it would shrink!" added Helen. Seeing Frances's face she continued, "Ah well, Ward 7 is an awfully busy ward, say you were so snowed under you just missed it among the other instruments." Frances smiled with a hopeless shrug. "Oh, come on, who cares, they'll buy another one" said Helen, as she walked on. "See you teatime."

Frances tapped gently on Matron's door.

"Come in" came the voice of 'God'. "Sit down,

nurse, and how can I help you?" Frances handed over the requisition form with an embarrassed smile. Matron enquired if she was aware that an article such as the horn should not go into the steriliser.

"Oh yes, Matron, it was careless of me. I was rushing. I am extremely sorry."

"Hum, take this requisition to the hospital secretary and don't let it happen ever again."

"Thank you, Matron," smiled Frances as she reached for the door handle. Outside the door stood Sister Williams.

"What happened?" she enquired of Frances.

"I have to take it to the hospital secretary, and I did apologise." said Frances.

"Thank heavens" said her ward sister with obvious relief. "I was afraid you might be in trouble, so I came to speak for you. You are a good nurse, though a bit too willing and gushing!"

Together the ward sister and her nurse made the journey to the hospital secretary's office. Fortunately he was able to supply another gum elastic horn from stock. Frances was much happier. Sister Williams was a lovely person. Frances's zeal and energy was often tiresome to Sister, who was very near retirement age.

Another day over, some study to get through, then an hour or two with Peter, perhaps to walk, certainly too late for any cinema. Peter was anxious to be married. Frances wished to finish her training first. She had no family to help her. She had very little money, and she knew the risk of pregnancy would disturb her training programme. The discussion was postponed.

Life on Ward 7 was an enormous help to Frances. She gained experience by going to Theatre and working in Post Operative Care. She gained in confidence and her sense of humour certainly developed!

CHAPTER SEVENTEEN

The new change list on the wall outside the dining room was lost in a crowd of bobbing white-capped heads. All eager to know their new assignments. STUDENT NURSE M. DONELLY - WARD 2 SISTER RAE! Frances walked into tea and wondered what life would be like on a Diabetic Ward, Female. She queued up with Helen and Noreen. Christmas was coming and they wondered if they could get time off together. Certainly Helen and Noreen would go home for a month to Ireland. Frances had nowhere to go. Irish nurses usually went home by boat from Holyhead to Dublin. Aer Lingus was for millionaires! Much was planned, but nothing confirmed other than study and more study.

Ward 2 was situated on the ground floor. There were 32 beds. Sister Rae was hardworking and strict with her nurses. Urine was tested three times a day generally. There were some patients who had to be tested on every opportunity. Gangrene was common, and at times patients were admitted in coma. There was much to learn. Many patients were short stay only. In for stabilisation, then discharged with a diet sheet.

Tedious as the urine testing was, it had to be followed rigidly. There were no litmus papers then. The Bunsen Burner was forever lit. The smell of urine filled the air! The cupboard that housed the various chemicals was nothing to be proud of. It was a mess of stains.

On Wednesday visiting was from 2.30 p.m. for one hour. Frances busied herself while the ward was full of visitors, cleaning the urine testing cupboard, rubbing and scrubbing with all of her might to remove the stains. The Ward Orderly was right, it was a waste of effort, she had already tried to clean them off - to no avail. Sister Rae passed by.

"Nurse, you will need plenty of elbow grease if you are to ever shift those stains", advised Ward Sister, and off she went to answer the telephone.

"Elbow grease," repeated Frances as she followed Sister, and patiently waited until she had placed the receiver down. "Sister, have we any Elbow Grease?" Sister Rae stared at her young nurse, and after a short delay answered

"Go over to Sister Williams and ask if she has any, and if she hasn't go and ask every ward, and be quick about it, but, if you are stopped in the corridor by anyone from Administration, don't let them know what we are looking for." Frances rushed over to Ward 7. Sister Williams was writing a report. Frances knocked on the half opened door.

"Ah, Nurse Donnelly, how do you like your new ward?" asked Sister Williams, with a warm smile.

"Very interesting, Sister, I'm enjoying it. But I am trying to clean a cupboard of chemical stains and Sister Rae feels that only Elbow Grease will do the trick, we haven't got any and Sister Rae wondered if you had any." Sister Williams assured Frances that the best idea was to start at Ward 1 and not to forget the Outpatients Department and ask everyone! Frances thanked Sister Williams and set out on her search for elbow grease. Convinced that somewhere in the hospital someone had elbow grease, she walked along the draughty corridor that ran through

223

the whole length of the old hospital. Ward numbers ran in even numbers on one side, and the uneven numbers in some order shared between the administration offices, and wards on the opposite side. Passing colleagues on her journey, and pondering on her search for elbow grease. In the distance she could see the Head Porter. Jim was an elderly man of many years experience as Hospital Porter. He was an Anglo Irishman, whose mind was a reservoir of knowledge, built up over the years from working among nurses and doctors, porters, clerks, orderlies and patients. He was a devout Catholic, and never failed to remind the young students to "mind their religion". Here's Jim, thought Frances, he'll know.

She waved to Jim a beckoning hand and Jim journeyed on towards her, weaving through Outpatients coming and going, nurses and doctors to-ing and fro-ing. She steered Jim to the alcove by the hospital kitchen and Jim, anxious to help, listened intently to Frances's requests. "Jim, Sister Rae gave me a hell of a job to do, and she reckons that the only thing to remove the stains from an old box is Elbow Grease. I can't find any. Do you know if the stores might have some?" Jim looked down at the young student with a smile that hid pity, and, eager to help one of his countrywomen, he said.

"They're pullin your leg darlin. Sure elbow grease means heavy rubbin, and hard work - not somethin in a bottle!" Frances stared at him, and all the energy drained from her. How could Sister Rae do such a thing! Jim gave her his handkerchief to wipe away the tears that filled her eyes.

"Oh Jim, I've been everywhere, they'll all be laughing at me."

"No they won't, and even if they do, let them see you laughing too. Even the doctors have tricks played on them, especially the students. Come on, back to your ward. Put it all down to experience and don't fall for any more tricks. Check with me first an oi'll put you right." With a fatherly wink he left her at the ward door. Sister Rae walked towards her with a wide smile.

"Any luck Nurse?" and Frances laughed and shook her head in a hopeless gesture.

"I've been everywhere Sister, how can I go to the dining room!"

"Same way I had to when I fell for that one 15 years ago! Don't worry about that box, it's an orderly's job anyway. Come and do the medicine round, glad you have a sense of humour, you'll need it a lot on this ward."

Ward 2 was busier than any ward so far in her training. Observation had to be 100%. Patients could comatose and quick action was needed to save life. Constantly reassuring concerned and frightened patients about their future health, advising them on the importance of keeping to their diets. Admitting new patients was a duty Frances had a keen interest in. Her depth of understanding the frightened, the worried, and the lonely was so deep that she often had to fight against herself to keep within the bounds of being objective and dispassionate if she was not to damage her own nervous system!

With all the great scientists in the world, and Government funds, could not someone work out the answer to Diabetes? Looking about the ward at all her lovely patients she glowed at the very idea that one day the answer would come and diabetes would be no more.

Six weeks soon passed and another spell on night duty became due. WARD 11 - GYNAECOLOGY: SISTER WESTLAKE. The patients were a cross-section of ladies from fifteen to fifty, and often older. A busy and lively time was the pattern day or night. Many of the ladies were in for investigative procedures and were not really ill or in pain, and when women were not in pain, and with time on their hands, fun and leg-pulling was routine. Whatever fun was planned or capers carried out on their fellow patients or on medical and ancillary staff, Frances found another channel of knowledge for everyday life. Anyone who spent time on Ward 11 positively developed a sense of humour or further enhanced their own gift.

Nellie was an older lady recovering from an hysterectomy and was awaiting discharge to the local old folks home.

She was a pet, and often a pest! Sister had Nellie's clothes locked away to prevent the patient from going 'walkies'! Every time anyone passed by, Nellie would ask

"Can you get my clothes love", or "Is there an 88 bus in there!"

"Not yet Nellie, they're waiting for a driver", or "Soon Nellie, soon".

All night long Nellie called for her clothes. The patient in the next bed to Nellie was about to undergo a vaginal examination. The bed was screened, the Gynaecologist was gloved, and the patient readied and Frances was in attendance on doctor and patient. Just as the doctor was about to introduce the speculum, Nellie reached over and slid back the screening and asked the amazed doctor

"Is there an 88 bus in there?"

"No Nellie, I'm expecting a large fibroid, I don't want to find a number 88 bus!"

Night time on any Gynaey Ward is as busy as day duty. Inevitably abortions were all too common, and were always sad occasions. Termination of pregnancy was a controversial subject. Frances belonged to the Catholic Nurses Guild in a very half-hearted way. The old trouble from schoolgirl days was still simmering somewhere in her heart. It turned her into a stone block wherever dogma controlled a situation. Other nurses on the ward had little or no trouble following the Guild's advice on termination of pregnancy. Frances felt that unless a baby was truly wanted by its mother then better that it was never born. She was wrong, of course, as she discovered in time. Many young mothers worried about finance, had good reason to think again about bringing another baby into the world of poverty, that she already suffered in. The mother-to-be with the fear of producing a mentally handicapped baby following her two previous pregnancies where a heartbreaking result ensued.

One night a mother of seven children had to decide between a termination of pregnancy or risk her own life. Father Shannon was called by Frances to speak to the patient. The mother refused to sign the consent form until her priest agreed that termination was not a mortal sin in the circumstances. Frances could only think about her own life and how important a mother was to the existing seven children. She was not allowed to voice her opinion. She listened with sympathy as the husband and his sick wife differed in opinion about the termination.

The patient was growing weaker, both kidneys were infected. The priest arrived. Frances received him warmly. She briefed him enough to enlighten him as to how seriously ill her patient was. The Gynaecologist's recommendation that a termination of pregnancy, then twelve weeks advanced, was vital to the patient's recovery, removing stress on the infected kidneys. The patient was torn between her respect for her religious beliefs and the risk to her own life. She was concerned for her seven children who were being cared for by her parents. She understood that the pregnancy aggravated her already weak kidneys. Her husband wanted the pregnancy terminated, and was much distressed at his wife's illness, and for his lovely children who could lose their mother.

Frances listened sympathetically to the patient and to the husband, but could say not a word to sway any decision. She pictured the innocent baby lying in the womb. Where was God? Why should innocent people suffer? The mother refused to sign her operation consent form until Father Shannon gave his opinion.

"I might die anyway nurse, even if I kill my baby" said the mother to her night nurse, and Frances's only hope was for some wisdom from Father Shannon. The priest sat by the mother and spoke quietly to her. Frances and the husband moved towards the ward desk. The little light above the patient's bed covered by a small green shade gave an eerie scene and feeling.

"We've enough children" whispered the husband to Frances, as if the innocent babe in the womb was something that meant nothing, unless it was held in his arms. But she couldn't blame the poor man. He was distressed and disturbed and beyond reasoning.

Frances kept her thoughts to herself and merely shook her head in sadness.

"I'll make a cup of tea for you and one for the priest as soon as the junior nurse returns" said Frances more to change the subject than any wish for a tea-drinking session.

Father Shannon joined them at the desk. He spoke to the husband within the nurse's hearing, but almost in a whisper

"I have heard your wife's confession, and given her a special blessing. She will be constantly in my prayers. I could not advise her to terminate her pregnancy, it would be tantamount to murder. God will make the decision. The husband was speechless with distress. He searched the priest's eyes for hope, but saw only tears of helplessness. The priest turned to Frances

"Call me any hour if you think Last Rites become appropriate." He declined a cup of tea. Frances escorted her hospital chaplain to the ward door. She could contain her feelings no longer

"Father" she whispered "If we do nothing we will lose mother and baby, and seven children will have lost a mother. Jesus was a man of commonsense, he moved with the times, he changed dogma where commonsense was needed. Jesus did not make the 'termination of pregnancy dogma', the Vatican made the law. These men could never know a mother's feelings, seven little children will have no mother, where is the sense." She dropped her voice to an almost inaudible level, but the priest heard every word.

"The patient may die, even after or during the termination" he answered. "Let God decide, let us trust in him." With the hint of a smile the priest walked out into the night.

Back to the patient and to the dilemma that faced all concerned, she bleeped the gynaecologist to explain.

Long before Frances completed her spell of night duty, the young mother lost her fight to survive. Frances found great difficulty to come to terms with that situation. She thought of the young mother. Was she brave, or brainwashed by Catholic dogma? She laid down her life for her religion, but lost the baby's life and left seven children without a mother. Life's problems were many, and that was indeed a sad incident. Where was the wisdom and the good in that whole event - Frances could not see. Maybe in time. She felt strongly in favour of abandoning all religion for one basic rule 'Do unto others as you would have them do unto you', and if that wasn't good enough, then what the hell!

Two nights off duty helped to release pent up feelings. To enjoy a little social life with colleagues, to see Peter, and for all to enjoy two nights at the 'Garryowen'. Hammersmith Palais was just along the road from the Garryowen dance hall, with the Police Station and the Fire Station situated between the two dance halls. Many of the nurses were going out with policemen and young firemen. The Garryowen had an atmosphere of such solid Anglo-Irish relations that no politician could be more proud. Except on a Saturday night! Irish lads would cross the road to St Augustine's to Confession. As soon as they had vowed to regret for the previous week's sins, they would tank up at the nearest pub on the corner of The Broadway, then, just before the dance halls emptied at ll p.m., they would make their way to wait for the girls! Fights would break out between the lads and escorts. Policemen, firemen and all would tackle and deal with them. The police van would pull alongside and every drunken lad would be thrown into the dark metal trap.

Although some bad facial cuts were often sustained on both sides, good nature and understanding prevailed. Saturday evenings were the best for the crowd and for the music. To stay away was to miss the best time in young lives. Everyone was happy. The priest heard more confessions than on any other evening! The pub made a fortune in selling the drinks. The young policemen and firemen and other heroes had their ego stimulated and satisfied, prior to escorting their ladies to their respective hospitals etc! The young drunks, educated for nothing better, lived to discuss their brawls next morning as they declined, no doubt, to take Holy Communion! Every Saturday night was the same, they never tired! Getting away from Hammersmith Broadway on a Saturday night must have resembled crossing London in the Blitz! It was terrifying and exciting. The young people dancing their way to the subways, the sound of horn blowing from taxis scurrying in and about pedestrians and drunks, covering the main road, usually in the pouring rain! Shouts of "Goodnight, see you next Saturday!" as parties separated into various groups on their way to the station. There was no 'really serious' crime, no drugs, rapes or aids. A girl could walk alone quite safely. The groups stimulated the barneys just because they saw another group, and seemed a fair side for a fight! Hammersmith Magistrates Court must have taken a fortune in ten bob fines on Monday morning!

The tube rattled and rushed along and carriages were full of happy young people.

A busy week lay ahead for Frances and her colleagues. Sister Tutor had set them some test papers to assess their progress in Anatomy and Physiology. Night duty gave them the opportunity to study, each morning until noon, then to bed until 7 p.m.

Night duty was from 8.15 p.m. to 7.30 a.m. The group usually collected in Helen's room for study and gossip. Tensions were released by 'talking over' problems and financial strain was eased by sharing whatever money they had, depending on the greatest need.

Helen and Noreen knew Peter and liked him very much. Maura, another colleague and friend advised Frances not to marry because she felt that Frances still lacked the ability to judge character and that Frances should wait at least ten years!

"No, no, no" exploded Helen one morning, "Peter is lovely, marry him."

Such times were fun, a lifetime before them, and their only worry was to reach their State Final Examination together. Night duty was ended with two nights off, and Frances moved to day duty on the Paediatric Ward. Within a week she felt that her real love in life was caring for children, whether sick or healthy. Her life found a purpose at last. The care of children fulfilled her life every day. There was so much fun with children. At quiet times she told them wonderful stories. Sick babies had her constant attention. The joy seeing them progress to recovery, and sadness at parting with them, was compensated by the parents' smiles, as they shook her hand and thanked all the staff.

The various personalities kept her entertained from a cheeky three year old, cute enough to know how to win attention from any member of staff with his

"I love you, have you got any chocklit?" all in one sentence, to the little girl who refused to answer any nurse, just kept her angelic face fixed in stare at a nurse, and only shook or nodded her head in reply. It got her everywhere and everything! The day of discharge proved how clever she had been. She chatted her head off then!

Surprisingly, day duty was followed by a further six weeks on the same ward for night duty. Frances was amazed but pleased. Poliomyelitis outbreak became a nightmare. Local Health Authorities all over Britain were ordering vaccinations. It was a very worrying time for all parents. Cases were being admitted at a rising rate. The Paediatric Ward was hectically busy. Little ones admitted with symptoms for investigation kept the Paediatricians on duty for endless hours, day and night.

One night, Frances was made aware from the duty book, that the Paediatrician, who was still on duty, had started 14 hours earlier to carry out Lumbar Punctures. She called the junior nurse to make a cup of tea for the doctor. Some time later Frances commenced the treatment according to the instructions left by the Day Sister:

1 = feed Baby Giles in Cot

2 = mother's milk in small jug in fridge.

Off to the kitchen to fetch the mother's expressed milk, Frances was baffled. There was no milk. Walking from the kitchen she enquired of her junior nurse whether she had seen any milk in a jug in the fridge.

"Oh yes, in a small jug, but I used it for the doctor's tea. I had a cup and I poured one for you and for the parents of the new admission!"

"That was the mother's expressed milk" said Frances, with a sickly feeling! "Go to Maternity and ask the mother for another jugful, about 2 ozs." A lesson for labelling any receptacle, thought Frances!

The early fifties were days when parents couldn't stay after visiting time. Every evening broken-hearted little tots stood sobbing in their little beds and cots after a much needed Mum or Dad had to leave when the silly bell rang out. It was not unusual for Frances to find an anxious parent or two hanging about the corridor while their little one cried loudly.

234

Frances had her own feelings about rules and bells!

"Come on in, and sit with your little one. If night sister visits, say you couldn't get away earlier from home, and you've only just arrived, and ask for five minutes." Before long the gossip spread to other mothers and Frances had more than her share of happy children and helpful mothers. She knew the day would come when that awful bell would be seen by the authorities for the distressful object it was.

The Paediatric ward duty convinced Frances that the most rewarding and enjoyable task in her life would be in caring for children. She intended to marry Peter. He was O.K. for her. He had integrity. He was kind and generous. He was industrious and ambitious. Frances was growing in self understanding, although she still had a long way to go in personal freedom. There were many times in her life that she felt immense gratitude to the nuns who had educated and cared for her. Fear and dislike for Mother Thérèse prevented her from making contact. The nuns were still a great influence in her life. In truth she walked through life, always in the Convent Shadow.

CHAPTER EIGHTEEN

By 1963 Frances felt secure and confident enough to make a trip to Cork City and to visit the Convent. She brought her daughter Colette, aged eight years, to share the moments. Over the years Colette had listened to so many tales of her mother's life growing up in Sundays Well. It was a first air trip for both of them. Peter willingly drove them to Heathrow Airport. He planned a weekend at home to decorate their sitting room.

Frances wanted a quiet visit. A nostalgic journey. On this first trip she would have preferred to walk up the Convent avenue, and meet no-one. To walk through the grounds, the playground, to visit the Bakehouse, to visualise Bunny and Mary and their old routines. To see Nellie's grave. To stand on the hill and to look down on the City. The sights and scenes were indelibly marked in her mind's eye. To lift the rusty catch that secured the latch on the Horse's field where the see-saw stood, A huge felled oak tree that lay across two old barrels, that held at least thirty youngsters, far too many for any form of safety! But there never was an accident in her memory. To bring to mind the screams of exhilaration and absolute delight as the big trunk ascended and descended. To hear Mother Brendan's voice warning them to take care and afterwards remarking that their guardian angel certainly looked after them! To stand in the playground where so much fun was enjoyed by all, racing and chasing; where little groups gathered to talk, out of the duty nun's hearing. Personal events that shaped their way of thinking. Experiences in fair play that controlled their view of everyday life. To see a small child observe the duty nun as a fox would his prey, until the Nun turned her back, then jump up to the forbidden tap and hang on, her weight making the tap sag from the old wall, and in drinking her fill soaked her blouse, and didn't care. Friendship, secrets and events in that playground constituted an education useful for survival.

The stewardess served a light meal. Neither Frances or Colette was inclined to eat. Colette had very mixed feelings. Mother Thérèse was no longer in charge, otherwise that trip would never have been attempted. Still, Colette expressed her view that maybe someone worse would be there! Yet again she would love to see the dormitory and the classrooms and see the chapel from where the children ran when they saw the kittens! All from Mum's tales.

Cork Airport was bright and welcoming. Gaelic language sited everywhere. Hustle and bustle and hundreds of travelling children fresh faced and happy all helped to give Colette and Frances a secure feeling. Frances felt proud for Cork. This was her first visit to Ireland since 1949 and all around she noticed success and achievement. Thousands of cars for hire and queues of people willing to add to Ireland's economy. There was no-one to meet the two pilgrims from London. Frances had arranged by 'phone some days before, to visit the Convent. The response from the nun had been warm and gracious. "Do, please come, we would love to see you", but the nun didn't give her name.

The airport is some three miles from the Convent and a taxi seemed convenient. However, perhaps there was time to check in at the Jurey Hotel to freshen up before the Convent visit. Colette was more settled and into the spirit of adventure by the time the taxi pulled into the Jurey's car park. Chatting with the driver on route from the airport of her intention to go to the Convent he excitedly told her that he was an Altar Boy during Frances's years in Sunday's Well. Frances felt exhilarated!

It was Saturday and the best that the hotel clerk could give them was a twin-bedded room with bathroom for one night. Frances accepted the arrangement and called Aer Lingus to book their return flight for Sunday evening. Thoughts were whirling through her mind. Would Mother Colette be there, Mother Agnes, Mother Philomena, Mother Good Counsel, Mother Brendan and so on? She talked to Colette, though constantly preoccupied with flooding pictures of the past rushing before her mind. Frances was capable of sudden calmness and control, that helped her to become objective. Checking her lovely young daughter was neat and tidy, and planning to head first to the nearest florist, they walked hand in hand to the taxi that waited outside.

As many flowers that filled the rear window space and half of the back seat, she bought with loving care.

"Glory be" said the happy florist, "Who are they for?"

"For the Good Shepherd nuns in Sunday's Well. They brought me up and I'm very grateful to them. I cannot think of anything else to give them." replied Frances.

"You know when I was a kid," said the florist "my Mammy used to say to us, If you don't be good I'll put you up to the Convent with those kids up there and you'll never get out!"

"Nonsense." said Frances, "It wasn't bad, we had our fun, we had the one old witch, but mostly the nuns were great, and I've come to no harm. I am a product of their upbringing, and now this is my young daughter, being brought up the only way I know how, the Good Shepherd's way! And she is a great kid."

By then the taxi driver and the florist were arranging the flowers neatly along the back of the car. Frances's mind wanted only to dwell on the good side of life at Sundays Well. It was a game she often played. Parting with illusions is a painful exercise. No medication can help. She would have to do it alone. The pain of questioning what seemed undeniably good and perfect, and by questioning what seemed sacred, by accepting being wrong, was still too painful to go through. Time would be the great healer, she hoped.

The profusion of colour among the various bouquets of gratitude added to the travellers interest in the environment as the taxi headed for Sunday's Well. Colette was silent. The car drove through the large gates and immediately in front of them was a large modern brick building. That was new to Frances. Left, and up the Avenue and not a soul in sight on a Saturday! Frances was excited but apprehensive. Colette smiled, the Convent and School gave a pleasing feel, the lawns were neat and the shrubbery in bloom. The month was May.

Somehow the avenue didn't seem so long as Frances remembered!

The travellers thanked the driver, and, with arms filled with flowers they mounted the steps that led to the famous large oak door. The door opened and before Frances stood Mother Otteran.

"Good afternoon" said the nun (famous for her bad memory!) and looking at the two visitors as if to say what do you want!.

"Frances Donnelly Mother, I've come to visit Reverend Mother." Frances spoke as thought she was talking to a patient on her 'District Round', with confidence and politeness.

"Come in, come in," warmed the nun looking somewhat bewildered, "I'll call someone" and she disappeared down the corridor. Frances and Colette found the situation worth a giggle. In no time Mother Philomena opened an inner door and the atmosphere filled with joy, and warmth of welcome and words that, although Mother Philomena was hugging Colette between the flowers, and the child, overawed at the welcome, dropped all the flowers from laughing. Nuns flooded in, Mother Brendan, Mother Agnes, Mother Colette, and "make way for me" came a voice that thrilled Frances, Mother Clotilde in a wheelchair! And she was followed by most of the nuns from 1950. Only Mother Finbarr was dead. Mother Coregia held on to Frances, she was thrilled with Colette as they all were. The nun from the Sacristy took charge of the flowers.

"Come and have some tea" invited Mother Philomena. Frances and Colette were lost among the group of nuns all eager to make their visitors warmly welcome. The table was laid with freshly cut sandwiches, Queen cakes, a gorgeous sponge cake and a pot of tea. The guests were seated comfortably and surrounded by warm and friendly nuns all eager to hear of every event in the life of Frances since she left them.

"Have another sandwich and tell us about Peter, where did you meet him, how did you meet him, is he a Catholic, how is Kathleen, do you ever see her, and your Father, did you ever meet him? Have another sandwich." Colette laughed so much seeing the first sandwich still in Frances's hand for more than 10 minutes!

"Ah, the tea, you've let it go cold" says Mother Agnes and promptly went off to make a hot pot!

Little was eaten and questions were flying about. Answers were hardly finished before another question! Laughter filled the air. There was not one moment of time for either guests to eat a sandwich between answers! Then Mother Philomena suggested a tour of the school building to show the changes, and as the hungry guests moved from the wonderfully laden table, Mother Colette said,

"They don't seem to eat much!!" Colette went into a state of collapse from laughing.

Mother Philomena and Mother Brendan took them on an exciting tour of new bedrooms with pretty drapes and lovely furniture, nice bathrooms. The huge old classrooms were redesigned into small sitting rooms and kitchenettes. What few children there were, were that day out shopping or staying for the weekend with Cork families. Their education was to the highest level, and the children were encouraged into commerce, nursing, journalism or whatever suited their own aspiration. The strange new building they noticed when their taxi drove in earlier that day was a new hostel. Mother Philomena explained that any sixteen year old who felt a need for independence was given a key to the front door of the hostel. There she had a bedroom and bathroom and the use of a lounge and kitchen with TV etc., until such time as it took for her to finish her exams and start a career. All education was given with other city children in the various schools in the city.

Weekend visiting with Cork families was encouraged and every effort was being made to better the lives of all children in their care. The nuns were dedicated to the welfare and future of their children. The nuns were aware that the past pupils had a very raw deal, and were very pleased that those days were over. It was impossible for Frances to nderstand the radical changes that had taken place, without remembering the magnitude of the coldness and the oppression of the old days. Convents are like any organisation. There are laws. There are also flaws. Closed minds that refuse to ventilate and change, but Frances found them to be a small minority. Mother Philomena was full of plans for the future. Never again would children be forced to act as maids and cleaners. Those tasks would have to be a young person's own choice. With the high standard of education available, every child's academic ability could be stimulated to reach any career. The nuns were happy indeed. Much had changed, and all for the better. Mother Philomena showed her visitors photos and slides of happy events since 1957, the year of the great change. Boys and girls were welcomed into care, whole families were kept together and the nuns studied for certificates in child care.

Frances was longing to ask questions about Bunny, Mary, Rosanna, Breda, Rita, Noreen Dullon, Cassie Hyde, Mary Laffan, oh, so many! Her mind was full of names. Rita married and was very happy in New Zealand. Breda was a nurse, with the Medical Missionary of Mary. Noreen was married, and lived very happily in New Mexico, Rosanna lived in England and was married very comfortably, with a beautiful little son. Mother Philomena gave Frances the address. Bunny was a nun, with the Little Sisters of the Poor in Southampton. Mary had visited and all felt as Frances did, deep gratitude. Her resentment to Mother Thérèsa's moods and punishments was still there, but Frances felt sure that in time, somehow, she would control that dangerous feeling that had taken up residence in her soul. Frances expressed her feelings about her relationship with the First Mistress, and she understood the loyalty of one nun for another when the answer she got was

"Ah, she meant well! " It was a closed shop and best left to history, but it didn't help Frances.

Mother Brendan escorted Colette everywhere, and a thrilling time was evident on the child's face. Stories told over the years came to life as Colette visited the playroom, as yet unchanged. The pigeon-holed cupboards were still there, though unused. The kitchen was the same. It still housed the huge Aga cooker that arrived in 1948 and it took all morning to drive the weight up the convent avenue on an enormous load-bearing truck. It journeyed from the north of England. The children at the time were 'gob smacked' at the scene. That gigantic truck with an escort of gigantic, hairy armed men who were equally gob smacked, being greeted by 100 yelling girls aged between 6 - 16 years! All waving flags and shouting hurrah! hurrah! The children had prayed earnestly for nearly five years for an Aga cooker for the kitchen nun, that would hold enough pots to cook lunch for one hundred kids!

"Aggie, Aggie, Aggie!" shouted the excited children, and the men beamed from ear to ear and threw sweets and chocolate to them. It took six weeks to install, and the kitchen was out of bounds and woe betide any lass seen near the men! Food was brought from the nun's kitchen until the day of the opening of the school kitchen. Joan Welsh, Bunny's sister, was in charge of the new kitchen during her year of work experience and it gleamed throughout. The splendid Aga cooker, a joy for the kitchen staff, remained hot enough, long enough, to melt the lumps of fat in the mincemeat! It was magic!

All too soon it was time to leave Sunday's Well. A memorable day for Frances and for her daughter. They had seen everywhere that Frances dreamed of. Little Nellie's room, with the tiny bed, the little shoes she wore. Frances and Colette signed the visitor's book. They were invited to return for lunch the next day and to Benediction before leaving for the airport. As the taxi drove them back to Jurey's Hotel, Frances knew that the first visit would lead to many more. A part of her had not left there, would it ever?! The faces and voices and events of the past, they haunted her every day of her busy life. The visit had been

244

enjoyable but it didn't cure 'the pull'. Nor did Frances want it to.

It was late for Colette when they got back to the hotel. A wedding reception had been in progress and guests were still drinking and celebrating in the lounge and foyer. The music was aptly loud and cheerful. Frances called room service. The tired pair looked back over the day and relived situations and laughed. Colette was not a Catholic and although she had utmost respect for the Catholic Faith, she was a little concerned about Benediction next day. Only from the point of doing the right thing at the right time. She knew there could be prayers she would not know - to join in, to stand up, or sit down, at the right time? Assured by her mother that it was a very simple service and quite short, Colette prepared for bed to rest for the morrow.

Lunchtime was twelve-ish and the guests were welcomed into St. Teresa's parlour. Relays of happy nuns surrounded them and Colette and Frances found a way to eat their delicious lunch, while answering many questions. Mother Clotilde was in great form, the wheelchair was no handicap to her. Frances assumed Tilly's feet were bad from poor circulation, that had to be the reason for the chair as the upper limbs were functioning perfectly well.

"You can wheel me into Benediction." said 'Tilly' to Frances!

The chapel was so beautiful. The guests were honoured with seats in the centre section, in front of the main altar. Colette observed her mother, in eagerness to do everything in order. Frances had taught Colette to respect all religion. Truly religious people took their rites of worship very sincerely and seriously. She saw in her daughter a lack of interest in a formal religious education, only because there was too much reliance on faith. Remembering her own problem as a child, Frances decided to allow Colette to read as much as she could, about Jesus's teachings, and answered questions honestly. Whatever religious discipline Colette adopted, as long as it brought the child happiness and fulfilment Frances would be satisfied. Holy water, relics and out-of-date words in prayers were not acceptable, and church or cathedral was visited purely from an historic point of view, just as were castles and stately homes. Girl Guides, Girls Brigade etc. were uninteresting to Colette. Too many silly rules with little reason! Visiting a convent called for respect for the belief of her hostesses. The organ music was heavenly, and Frances observed the magnificent altar. She joined in the singing and bowed her head in acceptance and respect during the blessing. The final hymn chosen by the music director - "Happy we who thus united" was sung joyously by all the nuns, the priest and altar boys and Frances. The atmosphere was electric with emotion for Frances. As she sang her mind held a vision of her school days in Church. She felt surrounded by a hundred and more children all singing with her. an incredible feeling of peace and joy and of being home.

The service over, the nuns accompanied their guests on a long walk covering all the grounds. The bakehouse was closed down. Bread was delivered from the city. The life was certainly easier by buying the bread! Though the lawn and shrubbery were kept neatly trimmed, the vegetable gardens and potato fields and greenhouses were all redundant, to ease the burden of manual labour, and to release the nuns to do the work originally organised by their foundress St Mary Euphrasia. The foremost duties of the Good Shepherd Order was working for charity. Listening to various accounts of the nuns daily routines Frances could clearly see, that though Ireland, was a country where religion greatly influenced everyday life, it still had its share of problems with alcoholism, drugs and violence. Inevitably women and children suffered. The Good Shepherd Nuns are ever ready to help them in their distress and danger. Homeless mothers, family conflict, marital conflict, conflict with the law, mental instability - all benefit from the relentless effort and interest of the dedicated nuns from Sunday's Well, together with a group of lay social workers and a battalion of wonderful volunteers in the city, including the glorious Legion of Mary.

"The world would be much poorer and at a great loss if we did not have the Good Shepherd Nuns," said Frances as she and her daughter settled down with Aer Lingus on their trip home to London. Reflecting on the volume of work the nuns did, she felt obliged never to let them down. To help others on her way through her life. Across the world, thousands of souls are living useful and peaceful lives, and will lead new generations to live happy and responsible family life because, somewhere back along the line, a Good Shepherd Nun and the Legion of Mary gave a hand in a time of crisis.

Little Nellie's room, with her picture over the bed. The room visited each year by thousands of people from all over the world.

Children Learn
What They Live

IF a child lives with criticism, he learns to condemn.

If a child lives with hostility, he learns to fight.

If a child lives with ridicule, he learns to be shy.

If a child lives with shame, he learns to feel guilty.

If a child lives with tolerance, he learns to be patient.

a child lives with encouragement, he learns confidence.

If a child lives with praise, he learns to appreciate.

If a child lives with fairness, he learns justice.

If a child lives with security, he learns to have faith.

a child lives with approval, he learns to like himself.

If a child lives with acceptance and friendship,

he learns to find love in the world.